BREAKUP
REHAB

BREAKUP REHAB

Creating the Love You Want

Rebekah Freedom McClaskey

New World Library
Novato, California

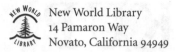 New World Library
14 Pamaron Way
Novato, California 94949

The material in this book is intended for education. No expressed or implied guarantee of the effects of the use of the recommendations can be given or liability taken. Although the stories told are true, names have been changed to protect the privacy of others.

Text design by Tona Pearce Myers

Library of Congress Cataloging-in-Publication data is available.

First printing, September 2017
ISBN 978-1-60868-489-2
Ebook ISBN 978-1-60868-490-8

Printed in the USA on 100% postconsumer-waste recycled paper

 New World Library is proud to be a Gold Certified Environmentally Responsible Publisher. Publisher certification awarded by Green Press Initiative. www.greenpressinitiative.org

10   9   8   7   6   5   4   3   2   1

Contents

Stages of Breakup

Inspired by the core concepts of AA and my numerous breakups, I wrote a new version of the classic twelve steps. These steps compose Breakup Rehab (BRx). Up until now, there is nothing like them that I've found that really supports people through the stages of breakup (as I understand them). Plus, there is no rehabilitation center that I know of or twelve-step program to hand-hold us through the suck. Okay, actually there are many options, but I didn't create them so they don't count. No one can give it to you like I will — the stages and the steps. Get your mind out of the gutter.

The stages of breakup (as I understand them to be):

The ending of us. The beginning of me.
Your ex turns into somebody you used to know.

Curl up in a fetal position and just need to be held.

Numb out by binge-watching TV.

Obsessively think about your ex and feel directionless without them.

Block numbers. Delete pictures. Return possessions.

Drink. Do drugs. Watch porn. Overeat. Turn to religion.

Search the internet for answers. Read articles on how
to get your ex back instead.

Lightly stalk social media accounts.

Consider therapy.

Sign up for online dating or load a dating app.

Start talking to strangers on these apps.

Stay distracted to avoid being sad and lonely.

Start reading self-help books. Or just buy a bunch
of stuff online that goes into a pile of things
you'll eventually get to — such as reading your
new stack of self-help books.

Endure the gap.

Go to yoga a few times. Think about eating better.
Actually eat a hamburger.

Implode into an existential crisis covered up by
being busy: Kids. Work. Money. Body. Yada.
Yada.

Start dating again.

Um, how well is that working? And we wonder why we
keep dating the same type of person that may be exactly like
our parents or a total reaction to how we were brought up.
I've been there. I get it. So I created the twelve steps of BRx
to get you through the stages of breaking up. To be honest,
this process wasn't all beer and Skittles.

Breakup Rehab was really hard to write. The first version of this book was a personal reaction to a few breakups, but one in particular. It was my adolescent attempt at redemptive self-expression. In this, my second attempt, I had to revisit difficult memories. The process of writing then editing this book was like a painfully awkward class reunion where I kept trying to look like the cool girl.

As I wrote *Breakup Rehab* I had to grapple with dispensing relationship guidance while being single, which felt like a twisted paradox. That being said, I've managed as a counselor to help veterans suffering with PTSD without having been to war. In this instance, if love is a battlefield, I've fought the good fight and know exactly how to help others navigate the land mines.

When you invest in creating something like BRx, you hope, as a parent does, that the failings of your past can be guideposts for others' futures. I have that special blend of life experience and academic training mixed with a philosophical mind and sensitive heart that helped me create BRx. I understand the struggle. I understand we all deserve the opportunity to be supported.

I remember finishing the first version of the book and self-publishing it over Christmas 2014. It took six months to complete the final edits and make one bad choice of a book cover — it looked like the zombie apocalypse — before I was "finished." Editing had kept me in a denial spiral about how I actually felt about my ex and my future. Ironically, that ended once the book was published. I then released everything I had been holding back in a rage that came out as a long and scathing email. I angrily wrote my ex everything that didn't make it into the book.

Rage, disappointment, hurt, fear, loneliness, uncertainty, and contempt poured out of me line by line as I constructed a narrative about our failed relationship. The book and the email were my attempts at catharsis. After I finished both, I thought the pain was behind me. Then in 2016 I got a book deal, which was awesome, but it meant reopening old wounds and facing new fears.

Reliving a breakup sucks. But it had to be done. This book was meant for me to write and to get it right not only for myself but for everyone trying to figure out how to create lasting love. In writing *Breakup Rehab* I discovered that you don't have to be special to help others — just real.

I poured everything I had into this book so that you could know that there is a guiding force in your life and a hand you can hold. I'm here to help you. No gimmicks. No pomp and circumstance. Just raw truth delivered as best as I can.

Sometimes I get academic when talking about love. Professor Rebekah will show up and dispense some wisdom. That part of me — the mentor — is totally accepting. Then right behind her will be "Screw it all! None of this matters anyway" Rebekah. That part of me — the rebel — is very confrontational. These two parts of me fight a lot. Maybe that's why I'm single. In any case, I use various voices when talking with you and sometimes at you, as a wise mother would. "Put your jacket on and call me when you get there. Don't text your ex!"

This isn't just another self-help guide. It's a self-realization journey. If I've learned nothing else in life, it's that the work is never done and the story never ends. Going through a breakup is all part of the process of being human. I'm here to remind you that you're not alone.

I want you to know for sure that someone in the world is walking with you. I constructed the BRx twelve steps with the intention to acquaint you with the idea that everything matters and nothing matters. To the person going through it, a breakup can feel totally significant. Realistically, most of the planet doesn't care. But I do. The silver lining to your breakup is that it can be a real shot at helping you learn what you need so that you can live the life that is meant for you.

Breakup Rehab is about cultivating balanced perspectives about relationships, life, breaking up, and starting over stronger. This is all part of a divine plan, but when going through a breakup it can feel like you didn't get the memo.

There is a pervasive idea that lasting love is the hallmark of a successful relationship. "To death do us part," right? Or when dating, it takes but a few seconds to spark our imaginations about our magical future and what could be created in partnership. After years of being a counselor and listening to countless stories of love and loss, I noticed a pattern — destiny.

A lot of us don't like the idea of destiny because we think it means we don't get a say. Some of us would rather believe that we can control the randomness of the universe through free will. The self-help industry was founded on concepts such as "manifestation," "Law of Attraction," and "alignment." As self-help guru Dr. Wayne W. Dyer says, "Change your thoughts and change your life," right?

My sense of it is that there are parts of our lives that

are already scripted. The choice we have is how we respond to the unfolding. How can we believe in "meant to be" or lean into the notion of soul mates / twin flames while in a relationship only to disavow the concept of destiny once a relationship ends?

Ahhhhh! This is less complicated than it sounds. Basically, destiny (as best as I can articulate it) is a guiding force. Think of your body as a blueprint of destiny. Your birthplace, race, gender, sexual orientation, socioeconomic status, and various other seemingly random factors set you up for a certain trajectory in life. I think destiny is the overlap between nature and nurture.

For instance, I think destiny guides us with the tools of inspiration, impulse, and that still, small voice inside that says, "Go for it." A lot of people take destiny to mean that everything is already mapped out and that fate has us by the short and curlies. I don't actually know the answer to that. But I do think we can perceive how we feel about our destiny, which allows for choice, decision making, and contemplation of our life path. We can have active or passive roles in our destiny contingent on our points of view.

But what about rape, murder, abuse, and evil? Is that destiny or is destiny just the good stuff? If you believe that we can't have light without dark, and that duality is our reality, then yes, our psycho ex or lost love is all a part of our destiny. It's a hard pill to swallow, but we have a choice what to wash it down with — fear or love.

We all have a capacity to realize who we are meant to be in this lifetime. Sometimes we are shown that by the people we love and who love us back. Sometimes frustrated love shows us who we really are. It's not a matter of chaining ourselves to an ideal. It's about dealing with what is as if you had imagined it — because you did. Your authentic self knew in the seat of your soul how it was going to unfold. Nonetheless, it had to and has to unfold. We can't know what we know until we go through it to know that we knew it — that is, life has a learning curve.

If something is meant for you, you can't miss out on it. If it's not, you can't hold on to it. Be at peace with who you are as the circumstances ebb and flow through you.

Don't worry, *Breakup Rehab* is not some heady book where you'll have to unravel the meaning of life. But I am going to make you work for it. I've added plenty of contradiction into the steps because life is messy and you have to figure out how to organize the mess in a way that works for you. In an effort to evoke your truth, I'm asking you to examine how destiny is playing out in your life while simultaneously demanding that you handle your business by giving everything you have into loving who you are.

The trend is to talk about "finding our soul mate" as being a part of our destiny. But when the relationship ends, we suddenly stop believing in destiny and start to think, "There is something wrong with me." Or if we ended the relationship, "There was something wrong with my ex." Or a variation of the two. Because breaking up is so complex and unique to every person, I did my very best to make the twelve steps simple, motivational, and applicable.

So who am I to guide you? I'm Rebekah Freedom. I love contrast. I like to play with extremes. I understand grief and loss. I have a master's degree in counseling psychology (FYI, for those who esteem credentials). I'm respectfully irreverent. And I've had plenty of breakups. But, most importantly, I'm going to help you.

I did my best to write this book as if we're having a conversation. In this conversation, I share insights into creating the love you want. I know your heart is hurting. In time, it will all be okay.

So as we go on this journey together, I want you to know I've got you. But since we don't actually know each other, I did my best to relate my story to yours. My hope is that *Breakup Rehab* helps you find your way home. My hope is that the concepts are simple enough to understand and profound enough to move you.

Thank you for collaborating with me in this process. I write. You read. Our hearts beat together. We move forward through Breakup Rehab into our new life, step by step.

INTRODUCTION

What Is Breakup Rehab?

To understand what Breakup Rehab is we need to understand what a relationship is. Essentially, when two people come together it forms a third energy or "entity," like blue plus red equals purple. Separately blue is just blue. Red is just red. Together, they're purple. But when blue falls out of love with red, gets interested in yellow (and wants to make green), then red is just left alone to its monochrome. I wrote this book for all shades and hues, for those who colored inside the lines and those who didn't even know lines were a thing. Primarily, I wrote this knowing that no matter if you're the one with the broken heart or the one who did the breaking, we all bleed red.

I understand that you've reached for this book because you want epic sex; because you want to wake up next to

someone who "gets you"; because you thought you had
that; because you realize you didn't but wish you did; because being single sucks; because being with the wrong
person sucks; because you had a friend tell you about this
book and you'll try anything; because drinking isn't working; because drinking is working too well; because you lost
yourself and want to find yourself; because you're tired of
dating apps; because you didn't know you could hurt like
this and you want it to stop; because you want to get back
out there; because you "want them back"; because the internet doesn't have the answers on this one; because you don't
know what to do.

Breakup Rehab is here to support you through your
process of emotional, mental, and spiritual recovery. It will
remind you to love the life you have. It will hold space for
you to feel what you feel. It will illuminate your unique
path. And it will help you navigate the uncertainty ahead.

The only thing that seems certain after breaking up is that
it hurts. And it hurts for so many reasons, some identifiable
and some irreconcilable. Further, it's hard to trust ourselves
to make wise decisions after a breakup. Parts of us that were
surrendered to love wall off under the weight of what feels
like overwhelming betrayal. Simply, the logic follows, "I chose
this and it hurt me so I hurt myself." Or if you're a self-help
groupie, "What did I do to attract this to me?"

Ugh!

A New Story

Take a deep breath. It's going to be okay. I know it doesn't
feel that way. I know that you feel numb, and under that

numbness there is a current. There is a hunger. There is a new chapter being written and, though it may feel as if the book of life has closed, there is more to your story. Your breakup is part of your script and it's a vehicle for your rehabilitation.

When reading *Breakup Rehab*, you'll begin to understand that what happens *to* you happens *for* you. Conventional relationship advice tells us, "Having expectations of another person is wrong" and "love yourself first." It sets us all up to think that there is a right way to love. Is there? Possibly. Did you fail to get it right? Maybe. Is it all a part of your story? Well, the breakup happened (or is happening), so definitely.

I wrote *Breakup Rehab* because I know how difficult, disappointing, and devastating the disillusionment of a relationship is. It takes courage to commit to a relationship and a lot of good support to heal after it ends. The BRx twelve steps have been written to guide you from where you are to where you want to be. This book is written as a love letter to all of us dreamers who refuse to give up on living lives full of lasting love.

The steps of BRx have a flexible quality in that each reader will experience the energy infused into each step differently. The original twelve steps of Alcoholics Anonymous (AA) dictate that you do them in order. That doesn't apply as much to BRx. That is to say, the steps are not tightly packed structures as much as they're medicine for what ails you at any given stage of a breakup. I suggest reading them in order first and then working the ones that work best for you. They will apply differently to someone who is fresh out of a relationship as compared to someone who has endured chronic heartbreak. Also, guilt, shame, and apathy have a way of taking hold differently for those who left the relationship than for those who are still trying to hold on to it. The steps help both the rejected and those who did the rejecting navigate life after breakup.

I'm sure there are factors that I wasn't able to factor in when writing *Breakup Rehab*. Though inspired by the original twelve steps of AA, BRx is not the same as AA. I don't think that love is pathological. Loving is not a disorder — though mental disorders can factor into the breakup. If we're love addicts, there is a twelve-step program that addresses that (https://slaafws.org). Certainly BRx acknowledges the roles addictions play in our romantic partnerships, but it's more focused on addressing the journey of emotional recovery after we complete the cycle of a relationship.

Much like AA recommends abstinence, I don't recommend jumping into a relationship after you break up, but I don't not recommend loving again when you're ready. Readiness can be arbitrary. Set and setting matter. Timing matters. And, like AA, BRx *works if you work it.*

No matter where you are in your recovery, you can expect the steps to guide you. They will be a refuge in the storm of swirling emotions that seem to be pulling you in all the wrong directions. You can expect BRx to be your personal Wizard of Oz journey to get back your courage, your brains, your heart, and your power.

Breakup Rehab is also an invitation to not take things so seriously. No one goes through life unscathed and there is not a cure-all formula to create the love you want. But there are some steps — twelve, to be exact.

How to Apply the Steps

How do you get the most out of reading *Breakup Rehab*? The short answer is to just read it. At the very least it will provide a much-needed distraction from the persistent clanging in your mind and the sharp pains in your heart. At the very most it will totally transform your life.

Breakup Rehab begins with letting go, which is the most blatant and difficult concept to digest because the breakup initiates the process of reassigning our role from *partner* to *stranger*. One day we were one thing and now our life looks totally different. We have an identity crisis when the person we knew ourselves as and the person we thought we would be is slammed up against the reality of not knowing ourselves without the relationship. This is what makes letting go so critical. It's not an exercise in erasing the mind. It's surrendering the agreements, oaths, and vows we had that created an identity that no longer applies. In letting go we create the space to reconnect to the person we have been longing for the whole time — our authentic self.

The quality of any relationship depends on how in touch each individual is with their authentic self. What is this magical thing that I'm calling the authentic self? It's you, Boo Boo. It's not your body. It's not your bank account. It's not your experiences. It's the thing that is experiencing all of this while also anchoring you in your destiny. It may not make sense because it's something the rational mind can't really understand. It has to be felt.

Forgiveness is a feeling. It's the sensation of release, being set free, and a lightness that comes when we no longer hold our ex, our parents, and ourselves hostage to the past.

When we forgive we can then better connect to ourselves rather than be walled off through judgments.

It's not easy to do at first because the torrid current of our desires keeps us swept up in drama. As an aside, I love it when I swipe through dating apps and guys write on their profile, "No drama," which is code for "I'm an emotional idiot." Drama is just this thing we create because we don't know how to relate to our authentic self. We externalize, gaslight, deny, project, manipulate, and mess up. It's all a part of the learning curve of life and, of course, relationships.

Knowing who you are, loving someone else, and really feel'n it requires trust. Trusting someone else can be the most challenging aspect of forming a relationship. Some of us trust too soon and jump in with both feet. Others hesitate and move into relationship like a teenager learning to drive stick shift — all herky-jerky. Then there are those stalwart souls who remain stoic and reserved, never quite trusting. The naive and the guarded bring unique baggage to relationships. We're as free as our most limiting belief, which is dictated by our ability to trust.

Once a relationship ends, it can be difficult to trust. The way to restore trust is through self-reflection. That being said, we all have blind spots. We all have limiting beliefs. We're all as sick as our secrets. I kinda throw up in my mouth a little bit when I read posts online that say things like, "Too many of us are not living our dreams because we are living our fears." I feel statements and sentiments like this are divisive and plunge us into contradictive judgment. The reality is we have both light and dark inside of us and I wrote the twelve steps of BRx to reflect that. Dreams and fears coexist within us and motivate us differently. The dream of having a rewarding and loving partnership can motivate us to sacrifice ourselves for a relationship. The fear of being trapped can motivate us to get out of it. But wherever you go, there you are — to the degree of how aware you are. The steps are meant to guide you to that here-and-now place inside of you by enhancing your self-awareness skills.

Now let me be clear, just because we're self-aware doesn't mean life is going to be all kittens and rainbows. We'll still likely have to endure pain as a part of our path. Don't punch me in the face when I get all Pollyanna about your breakup. I'm just aware that breakups happen "for a reason." Sometimes they happen frequently — to us (I'm in this with you).

Are you thinking, "What exactly is the reason for my breakup?" Why exactly would destiny, fate, God, or your body guide you to get into a relationship that would inevitably cause suffering and heartache? What good is pain? You've heard it before, "it builds character." Oh really? Does it? A lot of us think, "Screw being stronger for this. Give me the easy way out." Listen, between you, me, and the birds and bees, you have to learn how to love the life that is yours and not the one you wish you had. The intention of BRx's twelve steps is to remind you to do that.

When moving through the steps, you will know that they're working if they move you. Timing is everything. That means that you could read a step one day and get nothing from it. A few months could pass, and you reread it resulting in a "mind-blown" reaction. Desires for things to be different than they are can keep us from realizing all that we have. So don't be afraid to revisit the steps over and over again.

It takes repetition to receive because we won't receive what we're not ready for. Trepidation creates resistance to fully receiving and integrating what we actually need. Rather than be uncomfortable with what is coming up, we tend to run away, shut down, or act out.

Gawd! Been there. Done that.

When I was with the one I was sure was "the one," I had this expectation we could take on the world. We didn't. This ended us. I felt as if I failed at achieving redemption through relationship. The breakup meant having to once again confront my fears of poverty, lack, diminishment, and the almighty unknown. I know, I thought that being in a relationship would save me too. Raise your hand if you deal with fear by trying to control it. That's okay. The steps also address our need to control.

You're going to get through this. Breathe. Try something different this time. Give this process some space. Lean in to the sensations and the thoughts that arise in you. Watch them come and go. Before you know it, love will come rushing in where fear once stood. If that doesn't happen, call me and we'll talk about it.

MAKE IT A RITUAL

Some things are going to change. Will you change with them? Or will you resist and stay stuck in your old habits?

Once you get to the point of being able to really love you, things will start to pivot. I'm not talking about the "selfie," self-involved, cocaine-Buddhist, narcissism type of "love yourself." Start with the man in the mirror.

My mother, God rest her soul, always told me, "Look at

yourself. Recapitulate your actions and examine the impact they have." I hated hearing this as a teenager. But you know what? It worked. That phrase gave me permission to own my flaws and to amend my behaviors. That's what we're doing here, people — by "here," I mean here on earth, in our bodies, in our relationships. We're learning as we go to own our flaws and be brave and try again.

If you want to be brave and try again, get BRx under-way. Step by step you'll gain a greater sense of humility, ownership, strength, integrity, power, and, of course, love.

I encourage you to set aside blocks of time where you can just be with this book. I've heard it said, "It is not the things we run to that restore our souls. It is the things we return to." I suggest creating a ritualized practice around reading *Breakup Rehab*.

Prepare your favorite drink. Sit in your favorite chair. Wear your favorite socks. Take a hot bath beforehand and cover yourself with your favorite lotion or oils. Men, turn off your phones, the TV, the radio, the porn, and enter the silence. Women, stop texting your girlfriends, swiping through social media, updating your dating profile, judging your body for being too something or not enough the other thing. Put the phones away.

Create space.

Do this every time you're going to read the material. Train your body and soul to receive the blessings in this book by making a ritual of it. If you start to close off, simply whisper to yourself, "Barriers down." Consider the adage, "Fear is the only thing that gets smaller when we run to-ward it." Rather than use distractions to build walls against fear, use ritual to train your body and mind to receive the blessings that are here for you. Focus your attention on the steps.

The rehabilitation that is about to happen has been catalyzed by your breakup. But BRx isn't centered on your breakup. It's centered on you. This isn't a book full of gimmicks on how to get your ex back or how to be more attractive. The intent behind the steps is to facilitate you to live in harmony with your destiny. In this way, you will become fearlessly you. And there is nothing sexier than being confident in who you are. So before you begin diving into the steps — pause.

Plan your ritual. Gather all the components together that will support you in feeling good. Delight your senses. Drink plenty of water. Now relax into this journey we're going on together through the steps of Breakup Rehab.

BREAKUP REHAB

The Twelve Steps

Step 1: Let Go and Forgive

Step 2: Trust Your Authentic Self

Step 3: Make Wise Decisions

Step 4: Face Your Fears with Love

Step 5: Live Your Purpose

Step 6: Examine Your Judgments, Respond with Compassion

Step 7: Practice Humility and Gratitude

Step 8: Overcome Pride and Grow Forward

Step 9: Recognize the Strength in Your Vulnerability

Step 10: Maintain Your Integrity

Step 11: Own Your Power to Love

Step 12: Create the Love You Want

STEP 1

Let Go and Forgive

"Letting go means to come to the realization that some people are a part of your history, but not a part of your destiny."

— STEVE MARABOLI

S tep 1 of Breakup Rehab helps you begin healing and moving forward by learning to let go and forgive. Every breakup is different. Some hurt more than others. Sometimes one person cares more than the other does. A lot of us cling tightly to some semblance of connection and try to remain friends with our exes. Some of us are successful at it. But for the rest of us, it's not so easy. So no matter if it's been one day or several years since your breakup, right now we begin the process of starting over stronger.

Let's get some tools under your belt. As we move through the steps together you'll get guidance in how to use forgiveness, trust, wisdom, love, purpose, compassion, humility, gratitude, growth, integrity, truth, power, service, and connecting to your ability to create the love you want. We start with letting go.

Relationships are cycles — beginning, middle, end. Of course, relationships are an extension of life and life is reflected in our relationships. After a breakup, we retrace our steps. We cry, contemplate, cajole, contort, complain, and cycle around again. Each phase involves letting go.

The beginning of a relationship starts by letting go of being single. The end of a relationship is marked by letting go of being a couple. In every rotation we're given the chance to forgive ourselves for only knowing our biased narratives about love, sex, connection, and partnership. We see what we want to see and shut out the rest.

The narrative:

Here we are together. I want you to know some things about me. I might want you to know everything. Maybe even show me the things I don't know about myself. But only if you play by the rules. And I might want to know some things about you. I might want to know everything. I might want to show you some things about yourself that you haven't discovered yet. But I'm not going to play by your rules. I'll play along for a while. But first you'll have to unveil me because I'm hiding behind what I think I should be. I don't tell people that. I just expect them to know how to "get me." If you love me, you'll get me. If you get me, you won't leave — will you?

Then we have sex with each other. But being naked doesn't mean being vulnerable. Having sex doesn't mean being successful at unveiling our deepest desires. Our clothes may come off but our walls don't always come down.

Oh yeah, this is how we're dating nowadays. We get naked first and ask questions later such as, "Why didn't that work out the way I had hoped?" Each relationship is like a fingerprint. It's totally unique. Some begin slowly and end with an explosion. Others are fiery and passionate and end with ghosting. Either way, we must let go.

LET IT GO

Okay. So, let go. Simple enough, right? Ha-ha. I mean, what is there to hold on to anyway? I can tell you that when I feel the slightest twinge of rejection I go running to my oracle card decks and start pulling cards looking for insight. I don't want to let go. I want to know what is going on and what is going to happen next. Then, like any child of hippie parents, I pull out the sage, start speaking in tongues, and feverishly contemplate becoming vegan.

We all have our own brand of neurosis that makes the simplest thing — letting go — seem like mission impossible. That's a reference to the movie and I think it applies to our breakups: "This is your mission, should you choose to accept it...." You will self-destruct in five seconds.

Letting go and forgiving is the first step of BRx because the primary reaction to heartbreak is to wall off, throw a fit, become frantic, regress into an immature version of ourselves, beg, whine, blame, bitch, seek revenge, stalk, one-up, fall apart...I can keep going. Essentially we try to control what is beyond our capacity to change.

You don't *have* to let go. Go ahead and cling tightly to

all the points of view about who you are because of the breakup, because of the relationship, because of what your parents told you, because of what your boss said, because of what you think is the right thing. Spoiler alert: what you hold on to you get more of.

At the very least, it would be wise to acknowledge that you're being let go of. Both the person who ended the relationship and the person who got dumped are being released and relinquished. The forms, identities, and structures that were in place, that the relationship was composed of, are being reorganized.

Give yourself some grace because letting go is a process much like the stages of grief. The last step of grief is acceptance. You have to go through denial, sadness, anger, and bargaining before you get there. Letting go can help us effectively release all the automated and repetitive crappy stories we live with. Letting go means choosing acceptance of who we are instead of emotionally contorting to fit the judgments of who we think we should be.

If I were talking to you about letting go, I'd say, "Listen, man, there are about a billion factors that you don't have dominion over." But we want to have control over our relationships. I get it. When I broke up with my ex(es), I just wanted to do everything I could to recreate the magic. After a breakup, we generally want to speed past the pain and reinstate the pleasure. So the first thing we do after a breakup is use various methods to try to "fix it."

There are thousands of remedies that you can try in order to feel better, to get relief, and to heal from your breakup. You're welcome to try them all. But in this instance you only need to become an expert at one — letting go.

Letting go isn't about giving up something. It's about surrendering the barriers we build by holding on to how it was supposed to be. These barriers begin to come down when we take an honest inventory of our situation. Okay, so in order for you to really get this next part of letting go, I have to give a lil' Psych 101 lesson sampled from Harville Hendrix's Imago therapy.

The things that attract us to someone are the things we deny or hide in ourselves. I can't tell you how many men I've tried to mother because I feel as if I can't "do" life without my mother. I try unwittingly to force my relationships to conform to my lingering unmet needs. It gets ugly real quick.

As a coping mechanism, unflattering, traumatic, or uncomfortable events, thoughts, and points of view automatically get stored in our subconscious. Bringing them back out again is work. That is why relationships are work — they tend to shine a light on all our unprocessed pain. This next part is tricky, so stick with me.

Each one of us is already whole. However, our aversion to pain results in forgetting our connectedness. We then feel separated because the avoidance of pain takes precedence. The messages that pain is trying to communicate are suppressed, repressed, ignored, denied, or subjugated by circumstance. We cut ourselves off from our wholeness through this instinctual avoidance. But the body and mind seek to feel whole. Total numbness isn't sustainable.

We long for integration in the face of abandonment. Therefore all the places that we're unwilling to feel pain, we feel a muted version of it in the form of desire. Desire then becomes the guiding force for us to realize and release our pain because it can prompt us to choose people and situations that will facilitate new awareness. We somehow gravitate to partners and lovers who mirror the pain we wouldn't allow ourselves to feel.

Basically, your ex has all the qualities that you're unwilling to look at inside of you. We're attracted to what we wish we could be and think that we're not. The interactions that result in attraction are in fact open doors to learning more about yourself by relating to another person. This creates a feedback loop. Your breakup is shining a bright light on the beliefs that originated with the avoidance of pain, which then resulted in patterns of behaviors that tanked the relationship. In summation of our lil' Psych 101 lesson, we're attracted to people who give us the chance to process our unmet needs because when we're loved for the things we feel are our flaws, we feel whole again.

I'm sipping my chai tea right now and wondering, "Did that make sense?" I'll keep trying to explain.

We want things in other people that we won't let ourselves express. I dated an artist whose parents totally paid his way. I wanted that kind of support. I wanted to be able to run off at a moment's notice and be irresponsible. But, goddamn it, my parents died in their fifties and that meant and means there is no one to fall back on. It's all on me, which made a partner who could escape both attractive and annoying as hell.

You don't know me, so let me clarify: dad, heart attack at age fifty-three; mom, colon cancer at age fifty-seven. My boyfriend had both his parents, their money, and their unwavering support. When my parents died, I had their money — $200K. But I wanted to be my ex. Since I couldn't do that,

I tried to make him "independent," like me. My unresolved pain and lack of awareness was the thing that led me into and out of that relationship.

You see, it wasn't ever about him. I was trying to heal myself so I could do what I came to earth to do. My real breakthrough was when I realized that letting go of the pain had everything to do with giving myself permission to feel it rather than place blame on the events that created it.

I hope that whole explanation just got highlighted and that you wrote something in the margins like, "I'm the person I've been looking for!" I invite you to reframe your breakup as a completion of a cycle. We look for ourselves in others. When we feel loved, we are reminded that pain won't kill us. But the avoidance of it will destroy us. Forgiveness stops avoidance.

Letting go allows for surrender. Surrender creates a pathway for unresolved pain to be processed rather than walled off. As our pain comes into consciousness we may feel guilt for not knowing better or doing better. That's okay. You did what you knew how to do. Learn from it and grow.

Letting go will create greater self-awareness. New awareness requires forgiveness so that you can be released from your past.

FORGIVENESS AND HEALING

What is forgiveness anyway? I offer you this: *forgiveness is not holding yourself or another hostage to the past.* It means giving yourself permission to be who you are — a perfectly flawed human who had an imperfect relationship.

It's over. Everything you were building toward, the time

you invested, and the moments you shared stopped. Who is to blame? What is to blame? Is there even anything to blame? I invite you to invest less time in avoiding the pain by playing the blame game and more time forgiving yourself and your ex.

But how do you forgive someone who hurt you so badly? How do you even begin to be kind to yourself after making such a dumb mistake? Hey, at least you tried. You put your heart out there. You got hurt. Now you have some big decisions to make.

Allow yourself the grace to say enough is enough and start to construct new boundaries. Oh, boundaries. I can hear the Dr. Phils of the world using this word as a catchall. We've talked about dropping our barriers and not walling off. How can we do that and still have boundaries? What do boundaries have to do with forgiveness?

Well, we teach people how to treat us by how we treat ourselves. We learn how to treat ourselves by how people treat us. Letting go and forgiving can break destructive cycles so that we can have healthier relationships. Breaking destructive cycles is the same as setting healthy boundaries. So forgiving yourself and others is a healthy way to set boundaries.

If you're afraid to hurt your ex, if you're a people pleaser, then setting boundaries is brave. In other words, if it's over, let it be over. Bishop T.D. Jakes has a powerful sermon where he says, "There are people who can walk away from you. When people walk away from you, let them walk!... Your destiny isn't tied to this person who left, people leave because they aren't joined to you. You just have to let them go....You have to know when a person's part in your life is over so you don't start trying to raise the dead." Love won't leave or forsake you. Trust that losing a relationship doesn't mean you lose your ability to love or be loved.

Just keep surrendering the pain. Keep letting go. Keep forgiving.

Is this starting to sound like all the other books out there? Ugh, I know, right? But there is no way I could write this without including the timeless lesson of forgiveness. Without it, we don't get a chance to try something new because we keep trying to repair the old. You can't skip over learning to forgive.

The noun *forgiveness* means the act of pardoning someone or something. To pardon a sin is to have mercy on the sinner. A sinner is simply a person who didn't stick the landing. The verb *forgive* means to actively behave in a way that demonstrates releasing yourself and others from accusation, blame, condemnation, judgment, and sentencing. Can you imagine the freedom you can have right now if you don't make yourself or your ex wrong for what went down?

Do it. Imagine your relationship as one of many poignant experiences you'll have in your lifetime. To forgive is to accept that what has been done *to* you was also done *for* you. Your relationship was your experience to have and so is your breakup. In some ways, forgiveness is the acknowledgment that there is something bigger than your agenda unfolding here. Like, "Okay, universe/God/whatever, I don't understand exactly what is going on here, but I'm going to surrender my agenda and see what happens next."

Did you have an agenda in the relationship? Don't lie. Did you? Some of us feel bad about not being perfect (in everything we do) and that's why we keep trying to improve ourselves. But self-help is kind of redundant if you consider that what is happening is what is supposed to happen. The thing that needs to shift is our perspective.

Forgiveness requires shifting your perspective. The roots of forgiveness begin by naming everything just as it is and accepting the past for what it was. Name it. Feel it. Then take inspired action to change it.

INSPIRED ACTION

Do you know what happens after you let go and you forgive? Your life begins to change. Shit starts to shift. Old stuck patterns clear up. Then, like a winter's thaw, new life arrives. New possibilities spark the soul. Destiny coaxes you forward with inspiration.

To be inspired simply means to be connected and tuned in. "Like, dude, chill out and feel the vibes. Mother Earth is trying to talk to you." Imagine sitting under a redwood tree or a massive tree with deep roots and sharing in the energy of that. Start to imagine you're rooted like that tree. It feels good, right? Letting go will feel good. Forgiveness will feel good. And inspiration will feel great because we can surrender what was for what else is possible.

If we act from this place of connection then there is no other option but to forgive because we can see that the same pain we're enduring isn't ours alone to bear. We're all in this together. We all feel disconnected from time to time and lean on each other to restore that connection. I like to play "Lean on Me" on loop until I feel inspired enough to go to the gym or do something other than obsess about the meaning of my life. Music, dancing, and being creative go a long way in being able to let go.

Learning to let go is an ongoing action. In simple terms, it's a form of acceptance — if not the purest form of acceptance. You can let go and forgive in any situation. But both are skills that take practice. Like any skill, letting go and forgiveness take time to master.

On the onset of your breakup, forgiveness may not look like forgiveness at all. From the outside, it may look as if you're blaming your ex for the breakup or wondering, "How could I have been so stupid?" *Because he was hot. I was horny. I was tired of being alone.* Right?

It's easy to come up with all the reasons you got together but not so easy to explain why love slipped through your hands. A breakup can make you feel as if there is an automated tape playing in your mind. You spend endless days and nights imagining elaborate scenarios or long-winded conversations that could have led to a different outcome. The *what ifs* bang around in your mind like a shoe in a dryer. Reclaim your mind by letting go.

When going through my breakups, my ego was always like, "Yeah, they're uneducated and ignorant of their 'wounding'" — the pitfalls of being a counselor is that you're too educated for your own good sometimes — "and they're dumb and I'm right." But I still kinda wanted them to like me. So then I would start to work on "fixing" myself, which meant more education that lead to my mind running the show. The head can protect you to a degree but it can't connect you to your destiny like your heart can.

We can all be a little "Judge Judy" after a breakup by placing blame and finding fault. It's part of the deal. Giving and taking blame is all part of the healing process — yippee. Forgiveness is when you can finally allow yourself to feel the pulse of holding on and letting go without attachment.

Um, how?

Every time you're like, "I hate his face but I miss him so much but I just want to have sex" — forgive. Every time you're like, "That was the best I could do and no one will ever love me like that" and then you turn on sad-sack music — forgive. Every second you give in to worry, fear, or become overwhelmed by the pain — forgive. To be clear, when I say forgive I mean let go. Give up slaving away to create a new outcome. Ease up.

Your destiny has not and will not let you down.

You get to be pissed at this particular fork in the road because, let's be honest, this sucks. It hurts. It's painful. Hello, Captain Obvious, right? I know you know it hurts and other stuff. But when going through a breakup it can seem as if you don't know anything anymore. So I'm going to keep reminding you, step by step, of how amazing you really are.

In order to transform your pain, to let go, to forgive, to move forward, to be in allowance, to embrace acceptance, to motivate, to create better, to be your own person, to stand in your sovereignty, and to whip your ass into shape, you must look in the mirror and say:

> I did the best I could have done up to this point. I am not wrong. I am not bad. I may have not got what I wanted but I am not going to let that stop me from wanting what I have got! I am the master of my destiny and I design it by never

giving up my opportunity to choose differently than I have before. On this day I declare myself set free because I forgive all things and everything I let hold me back.

Are you starting to feel better? Good.

You still have eleven more steps to go. From here on out you're going to continue to learn the exact tools you need to choose better, be fearless in the face of loving, get *you* back, and create the love that you're longing for. Simply — Breakup Rehab.

STEP 2

Trust Your Authentic Self

"He who conquers himself is the mightiest warrior."

— CONFUCIUS

Step 2 of Breakup Rehab helps you connect with your authentic self. This is the part of you that will nurse you through being curled up in a fetal position into being able to confidently stand on your own two feet again. There is a big momma bear part of you that knows exactly what to do to take care of you. Trust it. The papa bear part of you is for fighting your battles. Your authentic self can be both.

Let's dive in with a lil' philosophy lesson, shall we? There is a *you* that's observing you. That's your authentic self. The awareness that you're observing you is called meta-awareness. Think of it like this: we breathe automatically, but we can also control our breath. Eh? Pretty cool and also necessary for mindfulness practices, which you'll need in order to access your authentic self.

Synonyms for the authentic self include the wise mind, the manager, Atman, Christ consciousness, dharma, and many others. In its essence it conveys the idea that we can surrender control to a force larger than our rational mind.

The authentic self is infinite and unchanging. The authentic self is the observer of our mind, ego, body, and being. Duuuuuude. For real. (I've clearly lived in California for too long.) Okay, so back to where we were: Breakup. Identity crisis. Confusion.

Don't you hate the feeling that your ex is doing, like, ten times better than you are? They're posting on Instagram great pictures of food — at the brunch place you used to eat at together. Secretly, you hope they choke on it — or is that too violent? Whatever it is you're feeling, you're going to need to feel it, and to do that you must connect with your authentic self — the observer.

The authentic self communicates through feelings. Our gut sensations and nonverbal communications create an intuitive pattern. Intuition is an inner understanding that the mind, soul, body, and heart are all connected. It links these parts of us together through something that feels like an inner knowing. It takes stillness to connect to this feeling and to listen to the authentic self. In a word, *meditation*.

The authentic self is like a professor who watches over his university students. Parts of our psyche are like those college kids. Some parts are bullies. Some parts are caregivers. Some parts are lovers. Some parts won't come out to play. Some party too hard. Some parts are evil. Some parts are good. The authentic self watches over all of them. Let's get the most out of this metaphor and say that all these parts of us interact in the classroom that's life — and relationships…and sex.

So here we are in the university of life, learning about ourselves. Then a breakup happens; it's like being given a test you didn't realize you had to study for. Each part reacts differently to the "final" of the relationship. Some parts scramble to hide, others fight, others faint, others freeze, and some get aroused and want to release the stress through sex. Breakups have a way of reminding us that we're not in control of every part.

The second step of BRx assures us that there is a force bigger than the sum of our parts that we can rely on — our authentic self. In other words, being in the director's seat is different than being the actor. It's a matter of perspective. Since you've mastered letting go by now — ha — then shifting perspectives should be easy, no?

It's going to take a little more finessing. That mind of yours is going to hammer away at the logistics of the breakup, how moronic your ex is, how bad you feel, or how guilty you feel for not feeling bad. We all need time to wallow and make bad decisions until one day, we just choose something else.

I've slept with *so* many guys in response to rejection. It just sort of happens, and dating apps make it really easy to do. So I'm not suggesting that — *poof!* — you get all Zen with your authentic self and then everything will be better. How rad would that be? I just mean that you know better and once you know that you know better you can know how to do better and do it.

Trusting your authentic self helps you do better and be better and feel better. In a small way, solving your problems helps to solve the world's issues. I guarantee that you won't get every aspect of life right. I'm clearly still learning that. Keep trying to trust yourself. Don't attempt to use Google to figure it out. You're your own Google. Be still and listen to your authentic self.

YOU GOTTA HAVE FAITH

So what is trust? It has been likened to faith. So what is faith? It's reliance on a divine promise. And what is that promise? It's something that gets broken when we break up. We feel as if we let ourselves down and were let down. All the hours invested in believing in something that evaporated just doesn't seem fair. Plus, our egos are pissed off. The pain of separation can make it feel as if we can't trust ourselves.

But what part of you is not trusting you? Do you not trust all of you or just the shady parts? Do you know how you stop overthinking all of this? Trust your authentic self, the part of you that remains whole no matter the circumstances. Take the observer's seat. Step back. Instead of scrutinizing every little detail or just checking out altogether, go big-picture on your breakup.

Think of your authentic self like a baseball stadium and your breakup like the baseball. Focus on that image. Is the stadium filled with people or is it empty? Is there a game going on or is there just a lone baseball lying on the grass? In fact, where is that baseball? In your hand? In view? Hidden? Journal what you notice if you want to. But mainly just be curious about the imagery.

I wonder if you're wondering, "Where is she going with this?" In a word, *gestalt*, an organized whole that's perceived as more than the sum of its parts. Your authentic self is the organized whole. The parts are all the elements of your "baseball" stadium (emotions, thoughts, and sensations). When you use imagery in this way to investigate your breakup, it can provide insights that shift you away from identification with your breakup into observation of the breakup.

For example, a classic gestalt technique is called the empty chair. Hang in with me, this is about to be a mic-drop moment. Imagine all the pain you feel and have felt leaving your body and taking shape as an energy sitting on a chair in front of you. That's right, all your pain — gone. Take a deep breath. Now you're in the observer's seat, looking at your pain. That's what the authentic self feels like. It's spacious and wise.

Mistrust of our mind comes from identifying with our parts instead of with the whole. That is to say, our various parts have various narratives such as "I'm not good enough," "I'm too much," "I'm unlovable," "I'm right," and so on. Rather than believe that you are these narratives, step back into your authentic self, the essential and eternal part of you.

Repetition creates trust. At first, taking a meta-view of your breakup may feel weird. But when we repeat an action over and over it becomes familiar. We trust what is familiar. We suppress, repress, run from, avoid, and hide from the parts of us that don't feel like the person we think of ourselves to be. But as you practice taking the observer's seat and trusting your authentic self, you'll be able to have more compassion for all your parts. Then they can come out of hiding.

The more honest you are with who you are at your core, the more you can trust yourself. The more you can trust yourself, the greater your awareness about how your relationship and breakup fit into the big picture of your life. Connecting with your authentic self gives you more of a capacity to heal and move forward. Mic drop.

CONNECT WITH YOUR AUTHENTIC SELF

Throughout this book I'll unveil parts of my story. I'm doing this because I hope it helps you. If it annoys you, I'm sorry. But I want you to know that I've done some really stupid things. I've made some poor relationship choices. And I've learned a lot from those choices, just as I trust you're doing right now. Sigh.

I got into a relationship where I was frustrated, mean, and hyperfocused on external circumstances. Both in words and actions, I was constantly conveying to my boyfriend that he wasn't measuring up. He wasn't enough. I wanted more. I wanted things to be different. I can't even count how many times I thought to myself, *If he would just change, I'd be happy.*

I wasn't making any money, so I wanted him to make more money. I slept in until noon, so I wanted him to motivate me. I even wanted his family to be more like mine. He told me that my constant pushing made him feel bad. He revealed that he felt as if he couldn't trust his thoughts or feelings because I was one of the many voices that was telling him what to think or feel. But I still pushed for him to have all the answers. Until I turned it around by doing what my mother always suggested — I "looked at myself." I became the observer.

I realized that I needed to be the change I wanted to see.

I needed to learn to take care of myself. Even though the immature part of me wanted nothing to do with taking care of myself, the adult me knew that if I didn't learn the lesson of self-care it wouldn't matter who I dated. I would always hear myself saying, *If he would just change, I'd be happy.*

So I turned my external focus inward. Through introspection, I looked at my motivations, my fears, and my words. Every time I was on the verge of thinking, *If he would just...*, I replaced it with, *If I would just...* And you know what it took for me to realize that? I had to break up with him.

I had to choose to do that hard thing that was the right thing. Did this mean I won the awareness race? *No!* It meant that I had to face my own stupidity. It meant that all my knowledge about what makes for a healthy relationship wasn't enough to stop me from choosing my ego over love. I found a man who I could project all my fears onto and you know what happened? I fell apart.

Oh yeah! It wasn't pretty. Plus, it was one of those extended breakups that took a year to untangle ourselves from because we kept having sex. In that year, my heart hurt badly. Fortunately I had some tools I returned to.

Per usual, I started by reading books on relationships. I pulled oracle cards. I looked for signs in what songs my Pandora station would play. I talked to friends who were fellow psychics and asked for insight. I got my uncle involved as a liaison between me and my ex. I pretty much did everything but trust my authentic self. I tried to do it "my way."

Proverbs 3:5–6 sums this up by saying something like, "Trust in the Lord with all your heart and lean not to your own understanding — because you're going to mess this up, moron" (BRx adaptation). I did, I messed it up. But as the last half of the verse actually states, "In all your ways submit to him, and he'll make your paths straight."

Through prayer, rituals, friendship, and counseling, I finally got to the point where I was able to forgive myself and let go. I was able to take the observer's seat and inspect my pain. This then allowed me to trust my authentic self. I relaxed into the idea that everything happens for my best and highest good. I just had to trust the process.

So I invite you to do that now.

Breathe. Inhale. Exhale. Awaken your authentic self by saying:

> I am not defined by the reality in which I live. I can and will choose again. I am greater than the opinions of others and will not bow to the critic within. I foolishly set my target on winning that which I desired. But now I realize the prize lives inside of me. I have made stupid decisions but I am not dumb. I will not remain prostrate on the floor as if my soul has left my body. I will get up. I will stand up. I will rise up. I will reach up. I will reach heights that I never believed were possible. I will be restored by the renewing of my mind. The thoughts I had yesterday do not determine my tomorrow. I choose to see my breakup as a chance to meet up with a new version of me. There is no obstacle I cannot conquer. There is no fear I cannot overcome. There is sanity in the restoration of my soul. I am blessed. I am wiser now than I have ever been.

Let these words guide you onward. Trust your authentic self on your path through Breakup Rehab.

STEP 3

Make Wise Decisions

"The simple things are also the most extraordinary things,
and only the wise can see them."

— PAULO COELHO

Step 3 in Breakup Rehab teaches you how to make wise decisions. Sometimes binge-watching TV is the best decision you can make. Hiding away for a little bit while you gather the bits of your tender heart can be a smart choice. Plus, *Friday Night Lights*, *The Tudors*, and *Mad Men* are supportive in their own way. And this step prepares you for when you're ready to get out of your pajamas and back into the world by showing you how to make smart choices and wise decisions.

CHOICE VERSUS DECISION

What is the difference between a choice and a decision? In a word, *awareness*. Choices are like playing the short game and decisions are long-game strategies. It's easy to see the immediate result of a choice but a decision happens over an extended period of time. Just like the authentic self is the representative whole of its parts, so too are decisions the amalgamations of multiple choices made over time.

Motivational speakers really get off on choices and decisions. I start my day listening to influencers such as Tony Robbins, Les Brown, Eric Thomas, and many others on YouTube. If doing this works for you, then set an alarm and give yourself thirty minutes to give your full attention to what these influencers are saying. A core message is, "Take responsibility for your life." It's hard being an adult because you're required to make choices and decisions, and to take responsibility. I can't think of another time in life when it's more difficult to do so than in a breakup.

After I went through my breakups, my ego didn't want to make any choices or decisions. I just wanted to give up. I assure you, giving up is not the same as letting go because giving up means keeping your focus fixed on external circumstances. We've got to strike a balance between inside and out.

The thing about making decisions is it often begins with making stupid choices. The good news is that you never run out of choices. I consider each choice like a mini experiment. Some blow up in our face. Some are inert. Think of the choice to break up, or the choice to agree to break up, or the choice to not accept the break up as a little experiment that accumulates into experiential wisdom.

If you add up all the choices you made in the relationship and during the breakup, mix in a little reflecting time with your authentic self, and sprinkle in forgiveness, then you'll be better equipped to make wise decisions. I think that making a wise decision is composed of two things: surrender and being intentional in choosing how you feel.

You can choose something and then change your mind about it in the next few seconds. But when you decide on something, you've made a commitment. Your authentic self knows that it's already done — you're invested. "It's happening!" is a key phrase I like to squeal in fits of joy. This exuberant expression comes from deep within my being as an acknowledgment that the very thing I've been asking for is in the process of unfolding.

Is this making you feel better or just more confused? I'm blending together such concepts as "ask and you shall receive," "change your thoughts, change your life," and "you gotta have faith." What if you're asking to get back with your ex but it's not happening? What if you're trying to focus on the silver lining but everything looks like shit? What if you just don't believe that things are going to get better? Then what?

Time is going to keep going. The person you want to get back is you. The silver lining will be revealed. Things generally get better. We may not know what the future holds but we know who holds the future. This is a religious sentiment and it applies here because, honey child, your breakup is not going to stop time. You gotta have faith that you'll be okay. So you better decide to pick yourself up, be brave, and try again.

DECIDING TO BE BRAVE AND TRY AGAIN

Oh yaaassss, child. Make this your mantra: *Be brave. Try again.* Decide to lift your hands up to the heavens and give it up. Decide that today is a new day full of new opportunities. There is no need to drag your past into your future. Your relationship may be over but you're not out of options.

Granted, breaking up can take a long time if there are kids involved, assets, and whatever you left at your ex's that is so crucial to get back. Deciding to be brave and try again doesn't mean that you try to get back with your ex. It could mean that, if that's what's supposed to happen for your best and highest good. As a word to the wise, you can't force these things.

Think about it. Are there things in your life now that you once prayed for? There is a phrase that describes this perfectly: "I still remember the days I prayed for the things I have now." Could your breakup actually be an answer to a prayer? What's the lesson in this? If we don't get what we want the first time we must be brave enough to try again. Keep after it. Feel your worth, your value, and your courage. Don't settle for scraps. Be patient. Get focused. Be assertive. (I'm totally cheering you on.)

While breaking up is devastating for most people, I want to acknowledge the courage of individuals who decide to leave abusive relationships, break codependent relationship patterns, heal from being raped, and turn the pain of molestation into activism, as well as those who are still teetering on the edge of breaking free.

Sometimes the choice we make to enter into a particular relationship turns into the decision we must make to leave it. Breaking up — it's not easy. But it's not worth your self-worth to hold on to a dysfunctional relationship.

If you find yourself in a dysfunctional relationship, take inventory of what role dysfunction is playing in your life.

Is it a familiar structure that echoes your childhood? Or is it that deep hunger, like an angry dog, that is barking and snarling at you to feed it the love it so desperately needs? We often don't listen to our instincts at the beginning of a relationship and only later recognize the accuracy of our own internal foresight. We have to go through it to know what we knew. This was true for Sam and Audrey.

Sam was a shy man. He liked drinking craft beer and binge-watching *Sons of Anarchy*. It had been a while since Sam's last "real relationship." Then one day Sam decided to get on a dating site and try to meet someone.

He met Audrey. She was a cross between a thirty-something professional and a tree-hugging hippie. They dated for a few months. Sam liked her, but he wasn't sure about their future. Of course, this didn't stop either of them from having sex with each other, which prompted Audrey to ask, "What are we?"

Sam didn't know the answer. Rather than try to figure it out, he cut Audrey loose. He chose to date her but decided he couldn't be in a relationship with her. So Sam resumed drinking and binge-watching *Sons of Anarchy*, and he stopped trying.

When I asked him why he gave up on Audrey, he replied, "I knew I wasn't going to marry her because the chemistry wasn't there."

A few weeks later Sam admitted to me, "I miss her."

Sam was ambivalent. Ambivalence is a bitch. When we're ambivalent we don't decide, we fall into the victim role; we give up. You see, the thing about making wise decisions is not to spend your life in avoidance or ambivalence. It's not about getting mad at men for being noncommittal assholes (which women can be too). It's about acknowledging that we all are learning as we go and it requires being brave and trying again — and by trying again I mean going after what we really want.

As the saying goes, "We don't know what we've got until it's gone." But once we know what we lost, we can get a better idea about the role we played in the outcome, and in understanding this we can be brave enough to go after what we really want. I know I've settled for approximations to what I really want. The list of what I actually want is long and detailed but best summed up as the echo of Brad Pitt's character in the film *Legends of the Fall*. While everyone deserves love, it's okay, and even necessary, to be selective about what kind of love we give to whom. We often only come to understand this in hindsight and through self-reflection.

Hold up. Let me try to get this out. This is complicated stuff.

We get wisdom through experience. Our experiences are guided by destiny. But how we feel about our experiences and how we choose to respond to our emotions are up to us. When we decide on something, ironically, it's an act of faith and surrender. We don't actually know the specifics of how to create a certain outcome. Rather, a decision is anchoring our trajectory.

The decision to break up changes the course of your life, and you don't know exactly where it will lead. But you *do* have dominion over how you choose to feel about the unfolding.

O Jesus, Mary, and Joseph. Feelings. Choices. Decisions. Destiny. Rehab. What does it all mean?

Basically, it's all going to work out. It *is* working out.

COMMITMENT TO THE WORK

Well, honey, you better *werk*. O sweet baby Jesus, rehabbing yourself after a breakup is work. Being you is work. Keeping your passions alive is work. Managing your schedule is work. Keeping yourself fit and attractive is work. Being human is work. And what do you think impacts the outcome of all the work you're doing? In a word, *commitment*.

Well, that's just cruel to bring up commitment in a book about breakup. Who do I think I am to talk about commitment when it's the furthest thing from reality? "Rebekah, I broke up. The commitment is over, lady!" Or is it?

I don't know. What do you think? Did your ex make you realize things about yourself that you were unaware of? Do you have…mmm…commitment issues? Of course. We all do. Avoidance of pain causes them. So all I can tell you at this point in our journey is that it's better to begin to commit to healing yourself than to try to squeeze commitment out of your ex.

Commitment is about constantly refining yourself rather than achieving — or trying to achieve — a state of imagined perfection. Every choice you make helps you in discovering what works and what doesn't. For instance, some people do really well after their breakup because they choose to hire a breakup and relationship specialist. Other people just need to travel and move out of the state their ex lives in. That's what I did.

I was like, "Byeeeee." But really, I was friends with my ex for several years, and every corner of Denver, Colorado, was filled with a memory of us. So I packed up my shit and moved to California. This was a huge commitment to my growth and healing. I'm not saying that you need to move to California — don't, there are enough of us here. I'm saying that making a decision to commit to the work of healing yourself is a wise decision.

You're now at the point on your journey through BRx where you choose *you*. Be brave and try again with an open heart and fresh perspectives. Gestalt your feelings. Get them out of you until they become something you observe rather than something you identify with. Journaling is a great tool to do this. By journaling I don't mean screaming into the abyss that is social media.

Get off social media — now. I mean it. Social media is a dumping ground after a breakup. It can be a temporary fix but you, honey, need a long-term solution. No good is going to come from mending your wounds with app dating, light Facebook stalking, or sending long-winded emails and late-night texts. *Stop it!*

Get your ass on a meditation cushion and attempt to meditate. Be with your body. Choose you!

CHOOSING YOU

Guess who the love of your life is? It's your body — a.k.a., the blueprint of your destiny. Your body is the one long-term relationship you'll have — from birth to death. Just think about the million things your body is doing for you right now. It's breathing, beating, digesting, feeling (so many feelings), and being pretty damn awesome.

You may be thinking, "Okay, good. So my body is the love of my life. But I hate how it feels right now." Chances are, you're in survival mode. It's overwhelming. That overactive brain of yours is trying to keep you alive by making mean-ing out of your breakup.

What's that about? Why do we need to make meaning from our experience? Well, there is nothing better to answer that question than neuroscience. The brain has three parts: the brain stem (lizard brain), the limbic system (animal brain), and the frontal cortex (the meaning-making brain). The lizard brain controls basic functions such as breath-ing and the stuff that keeps you alive when you get black-out drunk. The animal brain stores memories, hopes and dreams, and our fight-or-flight alarms. The meaning-maker part of the brain is how we sort wavelengths of sound into hearing and balance logic and creativity. (If you're a geek like I am, you can research this more by googling "triune brain theory.")

Everything we feel and don't feel during a breakup has to do with the brain-to-body connection. I could write a whole other book on this alone. Suffice to say, we store in our bodies what our brain can't process when we're over-loaded with emotion. A perfect example of this is the phys-ical sensation of heartbreak. For instance, the same part of the brain that lights up when we get physically hurt also lights up when we get rejected. This means that rejection physically hurts. But did we need science to tell us that?

I did. Knowing this then made me realize why I get so defensive when I'm rejected. Being hurt signals the *defensive* part of the brain that is like, "Time for a fight," or "Run!" Of course, it's more complicated than this because we all had different upbringings, which means we all have different baselines on how we react to trauma. Breaking up can be traumatic. It qualifies.

My parents were hippies, then ministers, then rich white business people, then poor again. They weren't into material things. I had an interesting childhood. Along with teaching me to look at myself, they also influenced me to take other people into consideration. When I get rejected my dumb brain tells me, "Be nicer to that person. They're sad inside and they're demonstrating that through their bad behaviors. They're just crying for help!"

Ugh. More on that later.

How are you coping? Are you in fight mode? Are you in flight? Are you aroused? How are you dealing with all this? I mean, thanks for reading, but when you put down the book how are you showing up in the world?

You may have already spent a great deal of your energy attempting to make meaning out of *why* the breakup happened — thanks, brain! You will survive. Cue the music. "Once I was alone…"

Healing is going to take some time. Get with the program and choose with your body, the love of your life. If it needs a nap, nap. If it needs to work out — you're not going to want to work out — just go work out. Choose with your body and in doing so you'll be choosing you, which is a wise decision.

ACTS OF WISDOM

Sometimes we don't know how we feel until we talk it out or write it down. Art and creative practices, along with prayer and meditation, reveal us to ourselves. The reflections we see can be integrated according to how receptive we are. Receptivity requires maturity and wisdom to know the difference between what we can and can't control (Serenity Prayer shout-out — if you don't know what that is, see page 177).

Writing is my pathway of knowing the difference between who I am and how I feel, which then helps me understand what I can and can't control. Sometimes I vomit onto the page because purging, although not an organized and controlled process, can be an integral part of the process of healing.

I've purged in my writing. I've written epic emails to my ex that seem more like PhD theses. I've written long-winded texts (that should have never been sent). I've written articles, letters that I'll never send, blog posts, and manifestation wish lists. In an attempt to cope with one of my more difficult breakups, I wrote a poem about trying to make wise decisions when the past keeps coming up again and again.

> *What remains is a shadow and vapor of song*
> *It hums to me in the morning and reverberates all day long*
> *What washed away in the flood now remains a tear on my*
> *   cheek*
> *I am stronger for the song, but in its singing I feel weak*

When I wrote this I was in that sullen place of being both angry that the relationship ended and even more pissed that I got left with a life lesson. I wanted to fix things so I could get back in the good graces of his loving arms. I even wrote an obituary about our relationship.

There are several creative actions you can take to get out of survival mode, writing being just one. I also encourage singing, dancing, painting, cooking, cleaning, archery, swimming, travel, attempting to be a vegan, and whatever else brings you bliss. When we don't do this, when we don't choose with our bodies, we tend to hate them.

The reason we hate our bodies is because we dump sugar, drugs, caffeine, and booze in them; we overstimulate them with electronics that keep us locked in fight-or-flight patterns. Ol' cliché here: we dump gasoline on a tire fire. We treat the love of our life like shit. "Damn it, body, why aren't you feeling like I want you to feel!" And it's like, "Give me some time, buddy. I just got emotionally T-boned."

So starting right now, begin to choose with your body. Drink clean water. Get outside. Get some sun. Go to hot yoga and push your edges. The limitations you're feeling aren't real. Keep calm and carry on.

You may never talk to your ex again, but you'll be okay. You may regret breaking up with the one person who "got you," but you'll be okay. Decide to nurture your body and use this tool I'm about to show you to soothe your mind.

Decide to be still. Collect yourself. Get grounded. Then use this process I learned during my undergraduate years at Black Hills State University. It's called D.E.S. script. Simply describe, explain, and state. For example:

Describe just the facts: We broke up. I'm still breathing.

Explain your requests: And I just want someone to love me.

State your feelings: I feel sad, alone, and afraid.

Write as many D.E.S. scripts out as you need to because they will help you chart your course and your destiny. They're also helpful when it comes to communicating your thoughts and feelings in a way that is clear and inviting to the person listening to them. For example: *We had sex on our first date. This made me feel like I really liked you. Now I want to get to know you better.*

Writing a D.E.S. script may seem robotic but it's better than, "I'm totally cool if you date other people. We should just be friends who fool around from time to time. I'm good with that because I don't actually *want* a relationship. So you go ahead and do whatever you need to do (while I secretly try to make you into who I think I want you to be)." Stop the cycle of lying to yourself and write your script so that your truth can be revealed.

Move forward by deciding to get off social media (for at least a month), go outside, get fit, practice D.E.S. scripts, and you know it — make wise decisions.

Also, say these words with me:

My life is not an accident. I did not come to earth to be less than all I can be. I am extraordinary in my ability to adapt. The dreams I dream have been given to me. I intend to be a gracious host to my desires for they are leading me onward. If I know better, I do better. It is with inspired action that I fill in the gaps of my life with purpose. I am on a mission. I have a vision. I am more than meets the eye. I am not defined by my six senses but by my uncommon sense. I have a path and a purpose. I charge ahead knowing that grace and mercy will be with me all the days of my life. It is not my breakup that makes up the map of my loving. I am a perfect representation of what is possible when you fail and try again. So on this day, I decide to use what I have been through to renew my commitments to myself: to stand in integrity, to be trustworthy, to love with all my might, to be a vehicle of transformation, to be a contribution, to raise my voice, and to honor myself and others with honesty always in all ways.

It's an honor when you honor those you love by never diminishing the light inside of you. You may fall down but you don't have to stay down. Get back up with Breakup Rehab.

STEP 4

Face Your Fears with Love

"It's hard but you have to tell yourself, 'It's possible.'"

— LES BROWN

In step 4 of Breakup Rehab you begin to face your fears with love. When we're single, we want to be in a relationship in part for fear of dying alone. When we're in a relationship we fear it ending. At this point you may feel directionless and all you can do is obsess over your ex. Or you may want to get as far away from them as you can. We run away from fears. We run away from the pain. But as long as you're running, run after your destiny by facing your fears with love.

What is fear exactly? Fear can take the shape of panic, anxiety, paralyzed will; being blocked, tense, shy, distrustful, insecure, timid, trapped, guilty, or paranoid. In short, fear creates the baggage we drag into a relationship. Conversely, love is nurturing, steadfast, trusting, open, uplifting,

holistic, and sweet, just to name a few of its many characteristics. Fears keep us self-serving and shut down. Love opens
us up and helps us unpack our baggage. So let's unpack
your breakup.

A part of being human is our biological imperative —
the need to breed. The cycle is fairly direct in the animal
kingdom: be born, survive, mate, have offspring, and die.
It's a little more complicated for us humans. We have educa-
tions, mortgages, careers, and various cultural pressures to
deal with. Many of us seek respite in the arms of a lover and
partner to help minimize the pressure.

What we can't do alone, we carry into a relationship.
Our unresolved pain becomes the baggage we must unpack
in order to connect to another. This pain can trigger our
fight-or-flight response, which shows up in behaviors such
as lying, hiding the truth, cheating, and being disingenuous.
Masking our fears perpetuates the pain.

REAL RELATIONSHIPS

We're becoming more and more isolated because of technology. We don't have to be uncomfortable or face our fears
because we have a Binky called a smartphone. Further, we
can become addicted to the comments and likes of "friends"
to validate us. We make snap judgments about a person
based on a single picture. Further still, thanks to dating apps
some of us turn a few lines of texting into a hookup. Ipso
facto, we become part of the porn industry by running away
from our insecurities and toward instant gratification.

Porn and the internet have changed the way we relate
to each other. Sex is a commodity. Digital interactions are

fantasy. A vast majority of us have our everyday lives and then the lives we post online. The culture of porn has become normalized through social media. I know that I'm guilty of posting sexy pictures and basing my value on my "followers." It's irrational and it plays to the primal part of our psyche. And given the endless options the internet provides, we can now have throwaway relationships.

Granted, one-night stands aren't a new sociological construct, but the speed at which they happen is. Hardly anyone pays for porn anymore as there are millions of free websites full of any and every kind of kink. It takes very little to no effort to be stimulated by two-dimensional images and use those images to get off. Sex addiction affects us all. When we overindulge in something that is meant to be sacred it becomes profane.

I'm writing this because I'm assuming you want more than a quick fix. You want to sober up — "get woke!" Your breakup can be a slap in the face to do just that — wake the f' up. But there are those individuals who don't want to sober up. They keep things on the surface, never knowing victory or defeat. The complacent, apathetic, and ambivalent acquiesce to banality. You get to choose what type of individual you want to be. Are you just a commodity to trade or an actual person to get to know? What type of relationships do you want to have, fantasy or reality?

Chances are you'll have several different relationships in your lifetime — the good, the bad, and the ugly. I'm not quite sure exactly which you just came from. In any case, you're single, and being single can be terrifying (you can't google your way out of this). I think the hardest part of being single is the isolation. And you know what people tell a single, isolated, lonely person: "You have to love yourself first before you can love anyone else." Gawd!

Yawn. That is such a worn-out idea. It's not a bad idea. It's just a little overused. It's like telling an orphan to parent themselves. Sure, they may figure out the skills to do that, but who are they going to learn from? Exactly — other people.

We learn to love ourselves by loving others, including pets. We learn how to love by watching others love. We are love. Love is infinite. Fear is our response to feeling separated from love. In fear, we respond through fight, flight, freeze, fuck, or faint. Our souls don't fear. Would an infinite being be afraid? No. But would a finite body with limited resources freak out when something is lost? Yes. So facing your fears with love happens at the intersection of where soul meets body — a.k.a., reality.

Soul Meets Body

I hope your coffee is strong and the force is with you. It's time for some more philosophy. What is a soul? Yeah, no biggie. I just asked you one of the hardest questions on earth to answer. You're welcome. Now you don't have to spend the next hour wondering what your ex is up to. I also want to acknowledge that you have a life of your own to live. I suggest spending it contemplating better things. Anyway, back to the question: What is a soul?

Your soul is infinite. We can't even understand what *infinite* means, but your soul is that. Okay, you're doing great. Stick with me.

What is a body? It's finite. It will be born, do some stuff in the growing-up period, and around "middle age" begin its long descent into oblivion. To be blunt about it, the body is a flesh suit.

Now contemplate this: An infinite soul is encapsulated in a flesh suit that resides on a rock that is hurtling through space. What is there to fear exactly? You might die? You most certainly will. You could age? That is going to happen too. That you're unlovable? If your soul is made up of love, because love is infinite, then what is there not to love?

In a word, *reconciliation.* We humans don't seem to enjoy the massive paradox of being infinite beings stuck in finite bodies. But, damn, have we done a lot in the last thousands of years to reconcile that through science, math, religion, philosophy, biology, chemistry, and, oh yes, romance.

Essentially all the stuff you're afraid of is biological. Your body is programmed to live, and pain is its warning system that it's dying. Tell it to chill. Even though your relationship is ending it doesn't mean your body is. All the stress you feel is getting projected in the future as anxiety, and the depression you feel, that's just your stress keeping you focused on the past.

Hello, infinite soul in a finite body who just went through this horrible yet possibly transformative life event called a breakup. Welcome to your life. You've got some options. Expand your mind. Choose love. Move forward. Skip the existential part of what it means to be human and just focus on the task at hand: face your fears.

How to Face Our Fears

To face your fears is nothing short of courageous. It's brave to work to bridge the gap between you and another person by choosing to surrender to love. It's brave to stand in the gap and close the door to a life you were wishing for. Facing your fears simply means allowing love to be your guide.

Our fear of loss, punishment, or pain can inform our choices. When I was seventeen, my father sternly told me, "If you get pregnant, don't come home." His words freaked me out so much that they influenced my choice to not have sex until I was twenty-two. Then I did have sex, and I liked it. I fondly refer to my twenties as my slut years, and I'm glad I had them.

(We'll talk about sex a little later. What is your relationship to it? Are you afraid of it? Do you feel connected through it? What is your relationship to your body and your orgasms? I mention it here because our sex life is one of the biggest places we hide our fears and act them out. Let's give that some space to air out. For now, think about all the ways your fears inform the things you choose.)

I can think of a grip of things I did in the last week because of fear. I work out because I'm afraid if I don't get abs I'll never find love. I avoid doing accounting because that means I have to actually learn about money and not rely on the manifestation fairies to whisk me away to the land of milk and honey. I wonder what would happen if I did my own accounting?

Anyway, how is fear driving you? What are you running toward or away from?

Here is a list of the possible ways that fear runs the show:

I wanted to make the other person happy (so that I
   will feel safe).
I needed to get laid (to feel desirable).
I wanted approval (so I can go on with life).
I wanted to fit in (because I don't know if I matter).
I needed the money (to be significant).
I like to help (because I can't receive).

Fear is about survival. It's instinctual to want to belong,
be recognized, be loved, be valued, be heard, be seen, and be
treated with respect. The thing is, our hunger — the beast
within — will take what it can get if we let it starve for too
long. It's always roaming and searching for its next meal as
a means of survival.

I'm not going to tell you facing your fears is easy. But
it's worth it. How can you feel safe now that you're on your
own? What can you do to protect yourself? How can you
have faith that you're worthy of getting what you need? Face
it. Ask the hard questions. Do your accounting.

The path to love has not been perfect. That's okay.

I'm proud of you for trying. You've come so far. You're
still here. Good job. Keep going.

That is largely what it takes to face your fears. Never
back down. Face your fears and name them. Listen to what
they're telling you about your needs. What hungers are they
expressing? Trace them to their origin and set them free by
saying, "I no longer need you in the way I did before." But
let's really ground this because I know that when I'm reading this type of book I just want someone to tell me what
to do.

This was me when I was going through my breakups:

Should I text him now or later? If so, what do I send? I'll just wait. I'll just get on Facebook — oh shit! There is a picture of him with someone else. Ouch! I'm going to call Sherri. She'll know what to do.... Well, that didn't help. She just told me to meditate. Now what do I do? Who do I talk to? How do I fix this?

I get it. In no uncertain terms, here is what to do.

First, *stop!* Push your big toes into the floor — do this barefoot if you can. Take a deep breath. Now inhale and look to your left. Exhale and look to your right. Keep pushing your feet into the floor with extra pressure on your big toes. Keep slowly swiveling your head to the right and left until you feel a sense of relief start to wash over your body. You can do this anytime a feeling of anxiety, fear, dread, remorse, longing, anger, rage, despondence, revenge, or sadness arises.

Second, don't text, email, snapchat, or send any communication over digital media. Just put it all in a journal. Don't put it in a journal, take a picture of it, and then text it. Just write down what you want to say. *That's for you*. Breakups happen for a reason. The relationship and the breakup were meant to be — both are equally important to your growth.

Third, as my friend Sherri would tell me to do, meditate. I hate it when I hear this because I just like to get amped on coffee and distract myself with other people's lives. But seriously, go sit down on a cushion with your legs in a relaxed position, support your back if needed, and close your eyes and breathe. Bring your attention to the breath at the tip of your nose. Then breathe. Your thoughts will radiate off you like heat off asphalt in a Texas summer. As you notice them, bring your attention back to your breathing.

This sucks, I know. I bet you still just want to fix it. Well, remember that fear is urgent. Love is patient. The challenge is in how we communicate love instead of fear.

COMMUNICATING LOVE

Fear makes us gullible. It makes us feel "less than." It sends our mind into a tailspin. We need healthy relationships in our lives. We need mentors and tools to teach us about courage, and there are some great examples out there. Who inspires you to be a better person? Hopefully, in addition to whomever you thought of, you also answered, "me." ("Me" as in "you" — but I'll take a bow.) How do you love?

One of the great tools of our time is the five love languages: words of affirmation, acts of service, receiving gifts, quality time, and physical touch. This simple rubric helps us identify how we express and interpret love. When I first learned of the love languages I thought the most interesting fact is that we often express how we love someone by how we want to be loved. If I know I'm loved by being given gifts, I often give gifts to show my love. But — and this is a big one — that is most likely *not* going to be how our mate wants to be loved.

Therefore a major step in facing our fears with love is to have a service-oriented mind. Remember, once we're willing to give love, we soon recognize that we're surrounded by love and it was only our fears that made us feel as if we didn't have access to it.

Asking how you can be of service to your opposite

doesn't mean you're a servant or that you lose your voice in order to please another person. It means that you take time to consider another person's point of view.

As a word of caution, it takes time to decode how someone feels about you via their actions. The deep pangs of starvation for connection we all feel can cloud our ability to be considerate. Instead, we take the stance, "Get it while you can." I've taken that stance. I'm not saying you should do that, but you might. Because I care about you, I'm giving you a gentle warning. Being in a rush doesn't really work out for the best.

Love can't be rushed. Learning to love takes time. It's new every time you meet a different person. Also, the psychotherapist Esther Perel has said, "Some people will have two or three marriages in their lives. Sometimes it will be to the same person." Love gives us room to grow. Fear, not so much.

Love needs to be fostered. Lust just wants what it wants now. I know a handful of people who will fall in love with a picture of a person, make up a story about how wonderful life would be with them, and then carry on a texting relationship with them for months. Fear can fuel lust. "It's now or never." "You'll never get another chance." "That's as good as it gets."

An online relationship is not a real relationship. I know that is harsh to say. But healthy relationships require human interaction, intimacy, a balance of togetherness and time apart, and commitment. Anyone can have a relationship with a computer. Some dating sites have even built in code that masquerades as actual women seeking relationships. People fall for it.

You're courageous enough to face your fears of being lost, lonely, too much, not enough, the cat lady, the outcast, or whatever it is you're fearing today. Fears are just smoke and mirrors anyway in this magic show called life. You're the master magician.

FEARLESS

If you're really committed to your rehabilitation, use step 4 to face your fears with love by mastering these three things: Master your thoughts. Master your words. Master your actions. In order to do this, take a moment — or several — to get in touch with the sensations in your body, that cauldron of emotion that is housing your soul. It's just a vehicle; it's not the driver.

As an example, "When I think about her I feel hot, flushed, and short of breath. When I think about being single I feel a tightness in my chest and I just want to lay down." This is what fear feels like — tight, restrictive, urgent, busy, hot, rapid, paralyzing, or numbing. Really tune in.

How do you listen to what your body is asking for? If it feels light and expansive, that is your body saying yes to the energy you're interacting with. That energy could be a thought, words, or an action. If your body is heavy, contracted, or feels confused, that is a no. Practice using the tool of feeling your body's yes or your body's no in order to master your thoughts, words, and actions. Using the evaluation tools of light and heavy is an effective way of connecting with your internal compass.

The work is to break down the barriers between you

and you. This level of self-mastery will rescue you from the depths of despair and restore your soul time and time again.

So let's practice. Repeat after me:

> I am solely responsible for my life. It is no one's fault that I am who I am. No matter the depth of my pain, the loss of my dignity, the weight of internal and external oppression, I will not quit. I will dance. I will sing. I will create art. I will let Spirit move through me. I will read. I will write. I will escape my captors. I will set slaves free. I will seek knowledge. I will learn the language of love, for fear will not be the frequency at which I reside. No one determines my fate besides me. I am connected to everything and my body is my own. I choose this one life to love with all I have, to be a vessel of truth, to expand beyond the borders of my imagination, to live in possibility, and to seek to understand how my actions create my reality.

Let today be the day you take action. Move your body — like, really move it. Break a sweat. Break down the beat. Clean your house. Clear out the clutter. Make room for fresh energy. And choose the love available to you through Breakup Rehab.

STEP 5

Live Your Purpose

*"If you can't figure out what you were meant to do in this life,
figure out what you were meant to do in this moment."*

— SHIRA TAMIR

Step 5 of Breakup Rehab helps you focus on living your
path with purpose. So often after a breakup we feel we've
lost direction. Our days and nights can be filled with repetitive thoughts about our ex. If only they would come back,
leave you the hell alone, be different, stop choosing someone else over you, and get with the program, then your life's
direction would be restored. Would it? Or is your breakup a
part of your path?

Let's start this step by bringing clarity to your breakup.
You may be wondering, "Why did this happen? What can
I do about it? What's next?" What if I told you that you *do*
have control over what happens, what to do about it, and
what comes next? That may not make much sense since I've

spoken about your breakup being a part of destiny. So allow me to clarify.

DESTINY HAS DOMINION OVER YOUR DIRECTION. YOU HAVE DOMINION OVER YOUR BODY. YOUR BODY IS THE VEHICLE TO REALIZE YOUR PURPOSE. Glad we cleared that up in all caps so that you could really get the point. You have some control but not total control. Your breakup is part of your destiny because it's sending you in a direction. You get to choose how to feel about it by being mindful of how your body is responding. The purpose of your life will be revealed through how *you* respond to your thoughts and feelings.

SCIENCE AND PURPOSE

Purpose is the thing we're meant to do in this life. Our occupations can be a part of our purpose. The things we create or bring forth into the world can be a part of our purpose. The children we do or don't have can be a part of our purpose. And the people we love and break up with can be a part of our purpose. So how does one live their purpose? How do you get a say over what happens, what to do about it, and what comes next? Take control of your mind.

In a stroke of genius, when going through the editing process of writing this book, I wondered, "How am I going to strike the balance between empowering my reader (you) to take action and getting them to accept what is unfolding?" Then I remembered Bruce H. Lipton's groundbreaking book, *The Biology of Belief*. Bruce explores the connection between mind and matter. The rudimentary version of his findings is that our thoughts change our body's chemistry and therefore directly shape our reality.

In order to bring clarity to your breakup and reveal your life's purpose, we're going to have a little science lesson. I'll keep it short and oversimplified. Quantum physics studies particles, matter, and wavelengths. Our thoughts can be considered wavelengths — or vibes, for the hippies out there. Our bodies are made up of particles and matter. They have positive and negative charges. Wavelengths represent the speed of matter — low vibration versus high vibration. Matter, atoms, cells, body systems, and the environment all interact in a symphony that we call life. A part of that symphony, which may actually feel like cacophony, is your breakup. Point being, mind over matter is an actual thing.

I'd like to apologize to the actual scientists who are reading this for my elementary distillations, but I do have a point. Our thoughts motivate our behaviors and our behaviors shape our bodies in an ontological loop. But we don't really know where thoughts come from.

Consider for a moment where the thought came from to fall in love with the person you fell in love with. Did you orchestrate that? Where did the inspiration to meet and come together come from? Further, who was the one who arrived at the notion that it was time to break up? Don't speed past this part if it doesn't quite make sense to you. I encourage you to go to YouTube and listen to hours of Alan Watts until you start to conceptualize that the creation of a thought is out of our control, but once that thought becomes conscious we can interact with it and assimilate it into a belief.

To review: We're souls in flesh suits. Our bodies are

constructed of DNA codes. In those codes we have an imperative to mate and create. Just as we don't know where thoughts come from, we don't really understand the transition that happens when a thought goes from unconscious to conscious. But I'll venture to say that that moment is what inspiration is. In that moment we feel compelled to act. Change comes in the stages of not knowing, knowing, preparing, acting, repeating, and refining. Did you get all that?

I'm really tempted to call all of this magic and be done with it. But I'm committed to helping you get clarity about your life, your purpose, and your breakup, so let's keep going. The part of you that observes you — your authentic self — can direct your thoughts so that you can manipulate the sensations of your body and decide on what happens next through your actions. You may not understand why your breakup happened but you can choose how to think and feel about it.

Did we arrive at a little more clarity? I think we got there. Whew. And, of course, there is more.

BREAKING UP ON PURPOSE

Your breakup is not an accident. You don't accidentally build a life with someone and then break up with them. You don't accidentally have hopes and dreams about building a life with someone only to go on, like, a hundred dates that don't get you closer to realizing your purpose. Ahem...dating is all part of the path too. *Living a life of purpose means living it on purpose.* Manage your thoughts. Direct your behaviors.

Destiny has dominion over the direction of your life.

You have dominion over your body by directing your mind. The synchronicity and magic you feel, the impulse to act on inspiration and then take inspired action over and over is how you realize your purpose. Purpose is a design for your life. Destiny is written in your DNA.

For instance, Jim Henson created the characters Kermit the Frog and Miss Piggy. What business does a frog have loving a pig? Think of Jim as destiny. Think of Kermit and Piggy's relationship as the response to destiny. I know they're Muppets. Duh. The point is that it was written for a frog and a pig to fall in love and have a never-ending romance. They fulfill that by interacting with each other. They take action on what was written. Are you getting it? We're almost there…let's keep going. There is plenty more to come.

AND ACTION!

Before jumping into action, ask yourself, "How?" Let the question hang there. Let it be a mystery. Let your mind wonder and wander as to *who you need to be* to have the relationship you actually want. Purpose is a blossom that was first a tightly wrapped bud before it unfolded in conjunction with the right conditions. How do you create the right conditions in your life so that love, healthy relationship, sex, and purpose are part of your path?

I'm pretty sure you're not going to find your life's purpose by watching hours of TV, working a job you hate, or hanging on to a dysfunctional relationship. The funny thing is, you *can* fail at what you didn't want in the first place. So you might as well go after what you truly want.

What you choose to focus on matters (science pun intended).

We don't have to know our purpose to live it. Experience often reveals it to us, and a breakup can be the unveiling. But we can't know what we don't know until we go through it to know it. So we may not understand how a breakup is a part of revealing our purpose until time passes.

Lord knows, after a breakup all we want is to get what we want. The desperate tears that baptize our face after having endured the end of our relationship that we never imagined can be a guiding force, sending us in a new direction. The pain of making the mistake of one-night stands over and over again can act as a foundation to set a new intention. The battle to be recognized and chosen by someone who will love us for who we are can set a certain trajectory. No matter the pull on your path, it's a path with purpose if you remember to be yourself. Being yourself is exactly who you need to be in order to live the life that is meant for you.

Some people are better at being who they are than others. My friend Sara totally embodies the energy of a hippie-singer-yogi-healer. She is an artist at heart, and being who she is helped guide her to Russ.

Sara is one of those girls who was given a name at birth and then took on a "spiritual" name that came to her at a festival. She studies yoga, massage, Reiki, and plant magic. Sara is also a decent guitar player and busks around town from time to time. As an outlet, she goes to ecstatic dance gatherings, where she gyrates and pulsates to tribal-fusion music with a room full of people doing the same. That's where she met Russ.

Russ is also an eccentric musician who had been single

for a long time when his path crossed with Sara's. They started collaborating on some projects, toured local yoga studios, and began to fall in love. Six months passed by and on a trip to Lake Tahoe Russ proposed marriage to Sara. The ring was meager but the gesture was huge.

They had an outdoor wedding in Oregon on the land on which they built their yurt. Their wedding pictures look like a scene from Shakespeare's *A Midsummer Night's Dream*. And they both brought baggage into the relationship such as financial issues, communication issues, and the paradox couples experience between masculine and feminine energy.

Over the years, I got phone calls every so often from Sara. Her voice would be distressed and she would talk about how "we almost broke up last night. The fight was so bad." I'd listen, and inevitably the hunger to connect with something greater would reveal itself. Her longing for a greater purpose than just being a wife lingered. Sometimes she felt as if she was losing herself to the relationship.

Sara and Russ were seeking meaning in each other. Marriage provided continuity, but somehow it also dulled their awareness of what really mattered to them as individuals. The advice I gave Sara was to reinvigorate things that helped her feel vital — to focus on her yoga classes, tinctures, nature walks, and such. When she tuned in to her passions she could bring more to the relationship and be less tempted to be defined by it.

In time, they both came to realize that they didn't come together to save each other. They came together to help discover and support each other's life purpose.

Russ and Sara are working out the kinks of sharing a life

together. They didn't break up…yet. Aw, too harsh? I mean, they might. They might not. But, you know, you broke up so let's focus on that.

Relationships can be difficult. Sara has wanted to bail on Russ at least a handful of times for a variety of issues such as money, mind-set, and sex-life doldrums. I venture to say most of us get into a relationship, forget we thought of it as a destination, and then begin to want something else. Of course, life naturally evolves. We go through cycles and rhythms.

Our body has a start point and an end point. It's the stuff in the middle that is a challenge.

You Have Magic in You

Why are breakups so challenging? Why is challenge integral to life? Simply, there is a part of us that is infinite. But in this body, everything is subject to experience. You can imagine anything, but to bring it into being is the challenge. Transmutation is magic. Thinking about wanting to be in a relationship and then meeting someone who wants to have a relationship with you — not just have sex with you and leave but who wants to walk with you — is magic.

We're all endowed with the ability to wield magic. We all have the capacity to channel the ethereal into the material. Our finite body only has so much energy in each day, so we get distracted. We get reactive to our environment. Wielding magic, which used to be called weirding, means we have to slow down and listen to the inspirations our authentic self is trying to communicate to us and through us.

We can't give what we don't already allow ourselves to

have, so what we give is also what we receive. What we do with our time and our body says a lot about who we are. I've heard it said that it's not that our troubles are so different. Life is life. It falls on the just and unjust. It's our solutions that are different.

REPURPOSE YOUR EMOTIONS

Life is propelled by the thrust of emotions. Relationships can give life meaning but often fall short of giving it purpose. Our emotions are often guideposts to exactly what our purpose is.

Emotion comes from the Latin *emovere*, meaning "to move out." Every emotion can be paired with a certain action. Some actions are voluntary; others are automatic, such as the survival responses of fight, flight, freeze, fuck, or faint. When we experience the despondency that follows rejection, our emotions, especially anger, mobilize us to get back on track.

Reflect for a moment on who you were before the relationship. Were you lonely? Were you desperate? Were you working hard at being independent? What qualities did you bring to the relationship? It's been said we all need the same basic things: to be witnessed, appreciated, and loved for who we are. Breakups have a quirky way of showing you exactly that.

They show you your ability to witness another person and all the judgments it brings up in doing so. They show you exactly how much you appreciate yourself based on the depth and breadth of validation that you required to feel what you wanted to feel. And breakups show you just how you define love. We don't know what we have until it's gone, eh?

In simple terms, you're *worth* being witnessed, appreciated, and loved within the safe boundaries of a healthy, loving, supportive relationship. No matter where you are in your journey, there is a way being made just for you — and your well-being requires looking at the nasty stuff.

LIVE ON PURPOSE

Think of the distinction between "I intended to do that" and "I didn't mean to do that." Don't live your life as if it's an accident. Your breakup isn't an accident. It's the result of a series of choices that led to a decision. So here we are. You're going to get through this. You may feel like a POW, but you're going to make it. Leadership expert Jim Collins gives us a great example of how.

In his book *Good to Great*, Collins tells the story of a POW named Stockdale. Collins asks the soldier two obvious questions: First, how did he deal with being there when he didn't know the end of the story? Second, who didn't get out? Stockdale's answer to the first question is, "I never lost faith in the end of the story." And to the second, he replies, "The optimists...died of a broken heart." Those statements are paradoxical. In the book, the author refers to them as the Stockdale Paradox. Yet in one sweeping statement Stockdale reconciles them both: "This is a very important lesson. You must never confuse faith that you'll prevail in the end — which you can never afford to lose — with the discipline to confront the most brutal facts of your current reality, whatever they might be."

I chose to include this story because it makes sense when applied to breakups. Like, "Yeah, I don't actually know the end of the story between me and my ex. There is a lot of stuff to sort out. But I'm not going to run from the current reality that we broke up. I'm going to face my fears. I'm going to get through this." Have faith in the reconciling of the gap between where you are and where you want to be.

If you've been practicing letting go, trusting yourself, and facing your fears then you can begin to conceptualize that you must have faith in the unfolding of your story while also being realistic about what is happening. Too often after a breakup we remain stuck in denial and blame. Break that pattern and take control of your thoughts. If you have a hard time doing this, move your body. Really living your purpose is not succumbing to self-pity but rather having compassion as you learn about yourself.

Over the course of your life there is so much learning to do. There are so many experiences to have. There are so many deals to strike. There is just so much. A breakup is an end, but it's not be all and end-all. The relationship you had is something you'll always have with you as you continue to walk your path. It becomes a reference point. If there is more to be learned within the confines of that relationship it will be repurposed.

The essence of BRx is to live with purpose. Although the sentiment is trite, it's true that you need to love yourself. That's part of it. But it's not the whole thing. Learning how to have a successful and healthy relationship can be a challenge. Our bodies are wired for attachment as a part of survival. Some of us have what is known as secure attachments, where we got our needs met as children and were able to grow and explore the world safely. For the rest of us whose parents screwed them up — thanks, Mom and Dad — we play out anxious-avoidant and anxious-ambivalent attachment styles in our adult relationships. Some of us cope with unmet needs by being fiercely independent and others by being clingy but not too needy.

Take this moment to look at your attachments. How did they contribute to your breakup? Integrate the idea that your breakup is a lesson along the road of your long life. Have faith that your breakup will make up only a fragment of your journey.

Think about it — the person you just spent a significant amount of time with, the one you now have to ascribe the awkward title of "ex," is an accessory on your path. Maybe there will be someone else who is better suited to what you actually need to experience. Maybe you'll have done some soul-searching and realize there is no one else you would rather go through life with than the person you just broke up with. Be at peace with your path. It's unfolding. Be mindful with your thoughts. They're here to inspire you. Be intentional with your feelings. They will guide you. Live on purpose.

Affirm your intentions and direction with me now by reading this aloud:

> I may not know what tomorrow holds but I know destiny holds my tomorrow. Living my destiny is the most intimate relationship I have. My life will not be recorded as an apology.

I gave what I had and what I had to give was my best at the time of its giving. Regret will not mar my direction but will make me circumspect in my reflections. Love is not lost. It is preparing a way for me. I am on my path. I will keep moving forward. I am a child of destiny. Tomorrow is a new day. I will rise with the dawn and I will invite all of creation into the mysteries that make me who I am.

You're worthy of what is being asked of you. You're worth loving. And you're worth the purpose you'll uncover when walking the path of Breakup Rehab.

STEP 6

Examine Your Judgments, Respond with Compassion

"Be curious, not judgmental."

— WALT WHITMAN

Step 6 in Breakup Rehab is the invitation to examine your judgments and respond with compassion. This step is universal to our personal development, which includes the stages of breakup. The heart can't heal in an environment of judgment. The mind can't be made clear if it's resisting pain. The body won't regain its vitality in an environment of condemnation and comparison. Realizing that your ex is no better or worse than you allows for compassion, which restores your soul and steadies your steps.

Let's begin step 6 with a brief religious study, shall we? Compassion is a fundamental Buddhist principle. Other religions refer to it as love. Essentially compassion can be defined as feeling strongly about the suffering of others as if it was our own. Buddhists adhere to the philosophy of the eightfold path to realize enlightenment and relieve suffering: right understanding, right thought, right speech, right conduct, right means of making a living, right mental attitude or effort, right mindfulness, and right concentration.

Christianity's seven virtues — faith, hope, charity, fortitude, justice, prudence, and temperance — are also applicable when it comes to practicing and applying compassion:

Faith is belief in the right things.
Hope is taking a positive future view, that good will
    prevail.
Charity is concern for, and active helping of, others.
Fortitude is never giving up.
Justice is being fair and equitable with others.
Prudence is care of and moderation with money.
Temperance is moderation of needed things and
    abstinence from things which are not needed.

The eightfold path and the seven virtues are like spiritual checklists. They help us to be circumspect about our thoughts, feelings, and actions. Compassion is an action. It has an expansive quality to it, while judgments are limiting and cause more suffering. So as you journey through BRx's twelve steps I encourage you to apply the eightfold path and the seven virtues so that you can examine your judgments and respond with compassion.

COMPASSIONATE BREAKUP

You did it. You made it through another one of my substitute teacher–like lessons. I only offer snippets of info in them because BRx could quickly turn into a PhD dissertation on the meaning of life. If you haven't caught that already, that's what I'm trying to weave into what is going on here. *The meaning of life is life itself.* We're here to give life to ideas, to create babies, connections, and inventions. Love gives us life. And breakups can shed light on the meaning of our life. Bring me a higher love, right?

Breakups feel like death. Can you think of another transition in life that's worse than a breakup? It can feel as if there isn't one because, unless they actually did, your ex didn't die. You have to live with the knowledge they're alive and don't love you anymore (but think you're a really great person).

Oh, how shitty is that feeling? "I totally loved you, gave you my time, built a life with you, and for what?" I'm grinning — so you could read *Breakup Rehab* and contemplate the meaning of your life. I told you this wasn't some heady book about the meaning of life — *it is*.

A breakup is an opportunity to truly pause and examine our beliefs about what we want from our years on earth. I hope you're brave enough to keep diving deep into the meaning of your life. The steps of BRx are meant to inspire you to ask the big questions, such as: What do I actually want out of my life? What do I want my legacy to be? Did I love well? Can I be brave enough to live with an open heart and peaceful mind?

But, you know, things are falling apart so there is more work to be done. Do you know what happens when things fall apart? We have a breakup-induced identity crisis. We feel formless and we search for new places to belong.

Hmm. Where might we look? The internet. You know what happens when we try to surf our feelings away? They turn into comparisons. Then comparisons turn into judg-ments. Then we mind-fuck ourselves.

GETTING JUDGY WITH IT

What is judgment? I'm totally judging you for not knowing what judgment is. It can mean discerning right and wrong. Buuuuuuuuttttttt…that's not what I mean. Let's say your authentic self had a message for you, such as, "Dat boy no good for you, gurl." My authentic self sounds Jamaican, so I made your authentic self sound Jamaican too. Don't judge. If you're judging yourself as a loser for being single — don't. Give yourself some credit rather than allowing judgments to distort your awareness.

Essentially a judgment is a barricade. We use them so people can't get in. And barricades keep us from getting out. But where do judgments come from? They're locked energy in our body from when a negative event happened and the body was like, "File that away!" They form as tools to protect our heart and mind from being hurt. They're like patches that turn into casts and sometimes full body armor.

I had an opportunity to participate in a workshop about how men relate to females. It sent all my judgments into high gear. It stirred my awareness that in order to feel safe I compartmentalized how I saw and interacted with men. As it turns out, I was operating from the judgment that men were stupid assholes who did nothing but let me down.

In this workshop I was provoked to yell, cry, and ex-press my rage for being constantly disappointed by the masculine; by my father and the subsequent men that fol-lowed. Then, in a moment of clarity, one of the men in the workshop said to me, "Maybe you're judging your feelings so you don't have to learn anything new about yourself." I had barricaded myself against receiving from men because I was afraid of them.

I had to admit to myself that I was judging men as wrong while also desperately wanting to be loved by a strong and loyal man. I was stuck in a paradox of wanting to trust but being so angry that I couldn't. I was trapped in my conclusions about men and in my judgments about how they hurt me. In that moment, I began to understand that healing lay just beyond the edge of my judgments.

In the workshop, I screamed all my rage out. But I had to be provoked and coaxed to do so because I had walls built upon walls. I thought, "Men let me down because I'm not lovable."

We often judge ourselves as nothing without someone. There is this notion in self-help circles that you must come to a relationship whole and not seek to be filled by another. But what is more whole than being broken, being honest about the "forever empty" we all experience at some point in our life that claws at our sense of self? I think being whole means being honest. You're entitled to want to have someone fill you up. You're entitled to want to feel that sweet release of being loved for who you are. Part of creating the love you want is to not judge what you want.

We all judge. We all have judgments against us. We all have been judgmental. Transitions — the end of a friendship, the death of a loved one, the disintegration of identity, the evolution of a career, and yes, your breakup — can be laden with judgment.

We judge because sometimes we don't want to know

what is going to happen next — unless it's going to be good. It's instinctual and corporeal. Judgment is instinctual in that there is a part of the brain that maps our memories, holds our hopes and dreams, and responds to internal and external stimuli to protect those hopes and dreams. Judgment is a survival mechanism.

For instance, think about having a suffocating mother who taught you to not express yourself unless it was in a way that pleased her. The pain of feeling suffocated can turn into the judgment of others who express themselves fully — "Who are they to do that?" That judgment was formed out of survival early on in your life. But you can change it if you're willing to examine it.

We use judgments to cope by labeling, reacting, and resisting the pain caused by breakups. Culturally we're taught that pain is wrong. It's shameful to need help. Shame keeps us stuck. We loop. We search. We google.

Judgments are our way of coping with being overwhelmed by our emotions. We stay at stop. Red lights switch on and off. But some judgments never give us the green light to move forward. We remain stuck. We remain buried in shame. We repeat old patterns over and over. We react. And we try to protect ourselves from judgments by being judgmental. The harshness of our pain is not from the pain itself, but from resisting it.

There is another option.

COME TO LIFE WITH COMPASSION

Numbness. We don't even notice it. Some of it is new. Some of it is crystalized. But it's here. Nothing makes sense after a bad breakup. Some things make sense after an okay breakup. The one thing that makes sense of it all is compassion.

Compassion is the ability to fully accept all aspects of ourselves and others. Compassion can be summed up in the words *me too*. It gives us the capacity to go beyond the rational world and access parts of us that just feel. Soon we begin to experience spaciousness around our feelings because they stop being sequestered to the confinements of good and bad or right and wrong.

The best way to understand compassion is to first review all the ways we resist pain. In an almost compulsory manner, we reveal ourselves through our reactions to our pain. For instance, I eat when I feel lonely. Then I think about the weight I need to lose to get a sense of control over my eating because I don't want to be rejected for being fat. Then I throw something up on social media about "trying again." All the while I just need to sit my ass on my meditation cushion and breathe. But we don't naturally Zen out after a breakup. We feel dead inside until sparks of anger signal new life.

I can't even tell you how pissed I was when I broke up with my first long-term boyfriend, Roy (who cheated on me while I was in the hospital next to my dying mother. Suck it, Roy!). There is this joke that goes, "What's the difference between a Jewish mother who cooks you dinner and an Italian mother who cooks you dinner?" The punch line: "The Jewish mother says, 'If you don't eat this I'm going to kill myself.' The Italian mother says, 'If you don't eat this, I'm going to kill you!'" Well, my mother was born in Italy and I'm half Italian. So let's say after my breakup(s) I was so angry that I was contemplating some version of a "cement shoes at the bottom of the ocean" scenario. Because I was able to harness it, my anger activated me enough to take stock of the situation. I figured out the kindest thing I could do was forgive because I didn't want to hold on to the poison of Roy's dumb-ass choices. Seriously though, who does that?

You might be pissed and thinking how crappy your ex is way before you get to compassion. That's okay — your ex is no angel. And get a grip.

Examine Your Perspective

Take a moment to examine your mental inventory of all the ways you were wronged by your ex. This is not a trick. Really dig into how awful they were. What's the worst part? What do you wish they knew about you that they somehow just didn't get? Don't hold back.

Now visualize putting your ex on trial. What would you be accusing them of?

"You ruined our family."
"You don't know how to love!"
"You're terrible in bed."
"You lied, cheated, betrayed me, and broke my
     heart!"

Imagine how it feels to be accused of such grievous offenses. Does it hurt? What is the person who is saying these things really trying to convey? I'm trying to get you to feel how it feels to be under harsh scrutiny. It sucks. So don't do that to your ex.

"But...uhhh...they really suck!" Let that go, babe. Choose compassion. I know it can feel counterintuitive because we want to be right.

We reinforce our "rightness" through righteous independence, rebellion, repression, seduction, acquisition, accomplishment, and distress. We all have an image of who we are in the world — basically good. But we're bad at predicting how others experience us. Therefore when we act in a way that provokes someone else to reflect back a thought or gesture that's not in line with our internal image, it creates cognitive dissonance. To protect the image we have of ourselves we project our judgments onto other people.

Before you keep reading, do me a favor, please. Stop being judgmental of your ex. Remember, they're human, like you. They have to negotiate life and for a while they did that with you. You had that. Now let go of it. Everything is impermanent. So you have a choice: you can drown in the waves of your emotions or you can learn to surf.

Don't judge me for that lame metaphor. Take a break. Get some water. Then come back and let's talk about compassion and your body.

COMPASSION AND YOUR BODY

I don't want to make compassion out to be a prescription. I'm not like, "Hey, dum-dum, just be compassionate. Duh." I hate when someone comes to a conclusion about my life and then just yells some spiritual jargon at me like: "COMPASSION!" "MEDITATE!" "YOGA!" "DO A CLEANSE!" For sure, do all those things. But don't do them to be right or to get life right. Do them because your body wants you to. Your body wants you to be healthy and compassion helps you do that.

Conversely, being judgmental can result in actual physical ailments. Unresolved emotional pain can become physical pain. In fact, by the time we feel physical pain, we've most likely been dealing with an energy imbalance for a long time before it manifests in the body. Some pain manifests immediately, such as the lack of appetite after a breakup, heartache, and brain fog. Other unresolved emotions have a more latent physical effect.

My sister was sick for a year after her horrific breakup that turned into compound grief because she didn't deal with my parents' deaths by getting help, as I did. She couldn't digest food because of undigested emotions from her past that she covered up with pot smoking. My friend who ended a four-year relationship with a man who she described as "selfish" got a horrible case of strep throat, which can be correlated to righteous anger. My mother who did everything she could to "keep it all together" died of colon cancer. Incidentally, the colon is linked to the psychological stance of being dogmatically positioned. My father died of a heart attack while having sex. He had intimacy issues from being molested as a child by his mother. Ironically, the thing he battled his whole life killed him. Unresolved pain needs resolution, and compassion is that.

You have a body. Your body is going to be your life partner. It's going to interact with other bodies. Though our bodies all look different, we share the essential quality of being human and wanting to love and be loved. Compassion allows for this exchange to happen.

THE ART OF GIVING AND RECEIVING

To review, in case you missed it, compassion can be summed up in these two words, *me too*. This means that we don't see others as separate from ourselves. We all have wicked shadow sides that, given the right circumstances, can do horrible things. Conversely, we're all humans doing our best. Compassion can be felt in the breath: Inhale renewal. Exhale death. The cycle of giving and receiving connects compassionate hearts together and gives respite to those who are walled off.

To receive is to die a thousand times to a resurrection of our heart and mind. *To receive* is a verb…as in a practice… to be openhearted and let love in. We must overthrow our judgments and allow ourselves to be curious about what could happen rather than stuck in the conclusions of what we think should happen. Practicing compassion means receiving each sensation like a cycle of breath. It comes. It leaves. Then there is another event, stimulus, person, place, or thing that comes in. Then it leaves. Receiving requires agility.

Compassion allows for that agility to become habit. Rather than run away from what we're feeling, we lean in. We examine it just enough to say, "Hello, I see you." Receiving means understanding that you're not isolated in your emotions. The sadness you feel, the righteousness, or whatever else is coming up from having broken up is not exclusive to you. What is exclusive to you is how willing you are to feel your feelings.

Did you ever watch that *Saturday Night Live* skit where Al Franken plays Stuart Smalley? Stuart is this self-help, self-affirmation character who has a show on public access TV. He begins his show with, "I'm going to do a terrific show today and I'm going to help people because I'm good enough, I'm smart enough, and, doggone it, people like me."

Well, good, smart, and likable people still do dumb shit. It's all a part of the process. We all sin and fall short of perfection, and then we pick ourselves up and "BE COMPASSIONATE!" I just did that thing to you that I hate when people do to me.

We do that to our exes too. "Be like this." "Do this." "Don't do that." "Lu-hu-uv meeee!" Luckily you're being compassionate to yourself, right? You're good enough, smart enough, and people (hopefully) like you. So do better. Think positively toward your ex and send love.

Sending Love

Sending love means thinking kind thoughts about your ex and your breakup. Imagine them doing well, being well, and feeling well. Access that place inside of you that knows as difficult as this is, good is here. It's not on its way; it's here now. If it's been years since your breakup, if you find that the baggage of the past is being dragged into your future, this gentle act of sending love will begin to lift the burden.

Your destiny is unfolding under your feet. It's offering everything you require to be who you really are. It's asking that you exercise compassion toward your judgments. Breakup Rehab is guiding you forward as a skilled artist of compassion and a master at giving and receiving love.

You're doing great. We covered some major ground in this step: a little bit of religion, an examination of our judgments, an old *SNL* reference, and taking the bold step forward to respond to your life with compassion. Keep up the good work! You're well on your way.

Find compassion for yourself and for your ex by reciting these words:

> Beyond the barriers of my pain there is victory. There is a heart that is fearless. There is a mind that is focused. There is a body that is forming into the best version it has ever been. I will not stop connecting with the most potent version of me. I will release judgments that are no longer of use to me. I will stand fully in the energy of grace and mercy, for I see that I am not so different from the one I parted from. I wanted to be chosen and so I chose myself. I chose to be the one who has my back. I chose to let the child inside of me know I will never abandon her or him. It is better that I try and fail and try again, for those who have given up on themselves have shown me that I do not have to fight for them. Asking for help is a noble gesture — it is an act of bravery. So on this day, in this hour, and in this moment, I declare that I will transform my suffering into strength and offer that strength as a gift to the world and to all who are ready to receive it.

We must take time in our lives to get right with ourselves. Ask yourself, "How can I choose what is essential to living my joy-filled life?" Send love. Practice receiving. Offer compassion to yourself, to your ex, and to the world by living the steps of Breakup Rehab.

Practice Humility and Gratitude

"There is nothing noble in being superior to your fellow man; true nobility is being superior to your former self."

— ERNEST HEMINGWAY

In step 7 of Breakup Rehab you explore how to practice humility and gratitude. This step goes along with the stage of breakup where maybe you're caught up trying to feed the hunger and thirst for connection with fast fixes. But the things we reach for that cause us to ignore our hunger create more of a problem. Maybe addiction was the affliction that led to your separation. I'm going to ask you to break the cycle. It's time to change. Once you apply them, humility and gratitude will get you through your breakup.

Humility and gratitude are two of the best companions we can have in the fallout of breakup. They're wise and supportive. They know when to slow down and when to start over. They have a way of assuring that our relationships are prosperous regardless of the outcome. Humility

removes the blocks we have so that we can connect to ourselves again. Gratitude then begins the repair work of healing the hunger by feeding it what it actually needs. Together
they address some of the core struggles we encounter when
going through our breakup.

HUNGER GAMES WE PLAY

I didn't read The Hunger Games series and I only watched
one half of the first movie. But I get the premise: kill or
be killed. In a breakup, this translates to try to look better
than your ex, be the first to date someone new, use your ex
for sex, and other acts of cruelty. It's hubris not humility
that many of us display after the end of our "forever." The
struggle is real.

The core struggles of a breakup include but are not
limited to shame, guilt, apathy, anger, grief, pride, and fear.
Desire can even be a core struggle because, well, wanting
something you can't have sucks so hard! Each core struggle
is rooted in being defensive. Humility is the way to correct
all of them.

Humility simply means you have nothing to defend.
There is an earthy quality to being humble that is very
grounding. One of the most humbling experiences we can
have is breaking up. Sometimes it's the separation that can
provoke humility. But most of the time it's coming to grips
with our ravenous hunger that is really humbling.

Think of all the places that your hunger for connection, touch, money, approval, and security has led you.
Sometimes that hunger can feel like the most biting loneliness. Sometimes that hunger provokes fear that causes you

to react by going on a date with yet another stranger who wants nothing more from you than sex. Or you isolate yourself and put on the mask that you're doing fine. Our brains are wired to protect us from real and imagined threats. It's not in our nature to do what is difficult, but we must. We must overcome our survival instincts with humility.

Let's talk about life as it actually unfolds. You have a story and I'm guessing it goes something like this. Sperm meets egg…that's too far back. So we'll skip over some of the details. You had parents. One of them raised you and one of them provided for you or it could have been a joint effort. If you're a child of a single parent, they did their best to raise and provide for you. While growing up, you learned how to trust but not how to handle conflict; how to be organized but not how to be emotional; how to be expressive but not how to be disciplined; how to get approval but not how to be confident; how to respect authority but not how to speak up; how to make friends but not how to keep them; how to be hyperindependent but not how to be a true companion; and the list goes on. A myriad of events contributed to shaping your personality, responses, and perspective of the world. The driving force in all of this was to find a place to belong so that you could survive.

Then, after the hormones hit, after the loss of innocence and childhood (which comes sooner for some than others), we all get the message, "Grow up." Then you do. You go to school, get a job, date, have sex, start to build a life, and then — *wham!* — you're confronted with the fact that you don't know jack shit about navigating a relationship, career, finances, home ownership, insurance, and the endless list of responsibilities that go along with being an adult. Now add a breakup to all of that.

Okay, so you survived childhood. No one cares. Then you become a teenager. Everyone is bitching at you to grow up. Then you prolong adolescence with college. Then you have to focus on making money. Then you have to start a family or whatever trans-poly-bi-wife-swap-fluid thing it is you're doing. The point is, it's pretty f'n difficult to learn to be humble when you have so much to handle.

Of course you're going to be defensive after your breakup. Of course you're going to want to wall off. Of course you're going to have trust issues. These are all normal things. It's totally normal to be sad, angry, numb, afraid, unhappy, lost, and compulsive after a breakup. What is *not* normal is to be humble.

Instead we treat our breakup like the Hunger Games — we weigh survival against love. By no means think I'm casually telling you, "Just be humble. What's the big deal?"

Being humble totally goes against our instincts. Love isn't instinctual. At least not the kind of love that opens our heart, surrenders our barriers, softens us, makes us strong in the face of adversity, and is the bedrock we build our life on. Lust is instinctual.

Lust makes us an object. Love makes us human. Lust drives our addictions. Humility allows us to love. What do you want running your life? If you said, "love," then be humble enough to admit you need help.

ADDICTIONS, LIKE HUNGER, DRIVE US

You can't write a book about rehabilitation without addressing addiction. We all have them. Some are dominating our lives. Some are so subtle that we call them habits or patterns. Regardless of their severity, they all share a similar flaw — the thing that is meant to treat the problem becomes a problem.

Addictions are the repetitive actions we engage in as an attempt to "fix" the hunger. Drugs and alcohol are insidious because what can begin as a prescription or as leisure can turn into a slave driver. Food, porn, lust, depression, sex, and many other "fixes" exist. Maybe that's why it's called "getting a fix." Addictions are complicated but they all have this in common: they don't satisfy the hunger. Rather, they starve it until the only answer is "more." You know what it takes to break your addiction? Humility — to stop defending.

Some of my most freeing moments happened when I was humble enough to admit, "I constantly feel misunderstood and this causes me to be really lonely." I came to expect that people "don't get me." I kept that a secret from myself for a long time and therefore would reach for men, clothes, body changes, and sugar to feed me. The moment I was able to admit that I craved attention, affection, and reflection, I began to heal my hunger. I began to shift my addictive cycle by taking a hard look at myself.

Reviewing my relationships was a major step in realizing the forces that were driving me. A little bit later I'm going to let you in on more of the details of the relationship and breakup that gave me enough insight to write this book. When I look back on it and when I look back over my life, it seems as if most of my failures came from my lack of understanding how to be humble.

Humility can bring you to your knees. It can make you feel small. I like to think of humility in the context of standing on the shoreline and gazing at the vastness of the ocean. It's humbling to realize just how small you are. Yet you are the ocean.

It's a paradox of scale. Feeling small can help you realize just how much you have because you live in a big world, how much you're actually supplied for. While breaking up doesn't make it easy to notice these things, it allows for the opportunity to relax into the fact it's not all up to us. Humility connects us with the forgiveness of letting go and to the surrender that invites in genuine gratitude.

YOU CAN'T BUY GRATITUDE

Gratitude is an acknowledgment of the vastness of possibility to which we all have access. I see self-helpers get out their gratitude journals and start scratching down phrases to manifest more wealth, such as "I'm so thankful for the million dollars in my bank account." There are stories of that working, right? Trust me, my journal is all about sex, naps, food, writing, and figuring out who I am, all crafted in clever phrases such as "I'm so thankful for my million dollars, all the sex I'm having, my super-flat stomach and yoga ass, and the man of my dreams." It's a fun exercise. Try it if you like.

It's not a requirement of BRx to make lists describing your ideal mate. I kinda hope you don't write down a bunch of conclusions about what you think your perfect life should look like. Rather, if you make lists, write down how you want to feel at the end of today. Then keep doing that for the next however long it takes to start feeling how you want to feel. Of course, none of us really want it to take more than a few weeks to get what we want, so we throw tantrums about it.

When I throw tantrums, I don't focus on how I feel. I focus on how I want others to make me feel. I'm like, "I just want a guy who knows how to go down on me, do my dishes, and pay for all my hobbies." I get really self-involved to the point of being selfish. I do this because I don't stop to be grateful for all I have and all I have access to. I start to forget that I'm a lady boss who has accomplished so much in my life. It all feels invalid without a relationship when I forget to be grateful.

I'm not telling you to sugarcoat your pain with gratitude. And don't shit all over the things you do have because of your pain. You matter, so take care of yourself like you do. Shift your perspective.

We made it. We made it to gratitude. I told you writing this was a beast. We've covered a lot of ground, right? And I'm setting you up for even more awesomeness. Thanks for coming this far with me. I got a little story to tell you, then I'll say some more brilliant stuff, I'll remind you of some things, and we'll wrap up this step.

Dan Broke Me Open

As promised, here is the story of, in some ways, what made *Breakup Rehab* possible. My ex's name was Dan. He knows I wrote about him and he knows he taught me the hard-won lesson in humility that "the only way out is through." He broke me open by being my perfect reflection.

We were friends for three years before we started dating. I met him at Massage Elements, where I was the receptionist and he was a massage therapist. I was smitten when I saw him. Dan is sexy. When we met we were both going through breakups. So we soothed each other by cuddling. But Dan, being who he is, would go MIA for months at a time.

As the years passed we got more physical with each other. It took two years of knowing each other before we kissed and three and a half years before we had sex. When I fell, I fell hard. We talked about marriage within the first month and a half of dating. I moved into his sister's basement with him and I tried to start building a life with him. But I couldn't.

He wanted to be an artist and I wanted to be a business-woman. But I didn't want to support him. I wanted to be supported. Dan wasn't good at adult things. He often lost things, which used to drive him nuts. Three months into the relationship I suggested therapy. He was like, "Why?" And, being a therapist, I was biased. "Because we need to learn to communicate if we're going to make this last."

The one place we could communicate was the bed-room. The sex was mind-altering. So that kept us together for a few more months. Then I couldn't take it anymore. I didn't want to live in his sister's basement. I felt like an orphan, so it was really hard for me to integrate into his family. After seven months of dating, I found a place of my own and moved out.

We fought more and more. Then he told me, "You make me feel bad about myself." But, goddamn it, I loved him. I was just trying to get him to see what I saw — potential. We couldn't make it work. I made one of the most difficult decisions of my life when I chose to end the relationship. I knew I was forcing him to be what I wanted and he didn't want that.

Dan and I broke up after three years of friendship and eight months of dating. It wasn't the kind of breakup you can categorize as clean. For one, we kept talking to each other. The attachment lingered long after the commitment had disintegrated.

Dan had a way of just up and leaving when things got hard. Or when things were fun. He was a gypsy-unicorn type whose parents footed the bill. He moved on with his life by doing what he always did — going on a two-month road trip and hooking up with like-minded pixies. When he came back, we slept together again. It was only then that he told me, "Sex doesn't mean the same thing to you that it means to me." That hurt so bad because not only had I lost my boyfriend, but I had also lost my dignity.

I kept trying to get him to be "my person." I knew beyond a shadow of a doubt that I wanted to be with someone I could commit to, someone I could marry — and someone who wanted to marry me. Because I was deeply in love with him, I wanted that someone to be *him*!

After the breakup I eventually blocked his phone number, but it wasn't enough. He threw a fit. Before long we were back in each other's lives.

We ended up dating again, seven months after the first breakup. I knew what I wanted, but in wanting it with him I compromised. I wanted back in; he just wanted to be friends with benefits.

Finally I got to the point where enough was enough. He was hosting a dinner party and I didn't want to be around any of his friends, not really because of who they were but because of who *I* was (or wasn't) to him. I wasn't his girl-friend. I hated the fact that they assumed we were a couple because I knew in my heart that wasn't true. So I lost it.

I told Dan that he was full of shit. His response was to let me know it was okay for me to feel that way. In that moment, I knew my convictions had to be stronger than my hope that he would finally commit to us.

We stopped with the back-and-forth and put the brakes on the bullshit friendship. I got quiet. I got humble. I sorted out what I really wanted — myself back. And I left behind what wasn't setting me free.

So that's the shorthand of the story. I saw Dan again a few years later when a tragedy brought us back together for a brief moment. When he came to my place in California, he talked about the woman he dated after me. They broke up after a year of being together and traveling the world. Dan told me, "Now I know how you felt." Somehow it didn't make me feel better that someone else broke his heart. I wanted to be the one to smash it into a thousand pieces.

I didn't say that, though. I went into "mom" mode. Got him dinner. Warmed the sauna for him. Rubbed his back. Listened to him talk about his loss. Then when he was getting ready to go, I hugged him and thanked him for all he taught me. I was really humbled by the relationship we had because I got to see that as much as I like to think of myself as a rational person, I'm not. Love drives me mad. I share this because I imagine you can relate.

Seeing Dan again made me realize that neither of us had fundamentally changed. We still were at our core the unicorn and the warrior princess. But life looked different on us. We had been weathered by the battering of moving, travel, breakups, and trying again. From friendship to re-union, the whole process was 100 percent humbling because I saw myself in another — and it broke both of us open.

CONTROL YOUR MIND

You can't control your ex's behavior. You never could. Even if you think it's in their best interest, trying to control another's behavior is manipulative, and it reflects more on you than on them. A controlling partner is often cause for a breakup.

Your ego, or conception of yourself, is most likely cracked, if not shattered. In your effort to regain a sense of stability, you may behave and communicate in ways that look like attempts to control outcomes. Why is that?

It's in our nature to learn. We also learn our way into patterns of speech, physical tics, routines, habits, and other automatic responses that manifest as repetitive behaviors. Patterns create blueprints called neuropathways on the brain. Just as highways make travel more efficient, our brain blueprints increase our speed in information processing, re-action, and response.

The things you and your ex did together created blue-prints not only on your brain but also on your heart, and it's uncomfortable to step out of them. I was friends with Dan for three years before we decided to date (and destroy our friendship). In that time, we created memories in every cor-ner of Denver — we made a blueprint of the city together. After our breakup I decided to move to California. I was like, "I don't even want to be in the same state as you."

Yeah, this dude was the dude who I "wanted to be like"

(adult tantrum voice). "Eh, Dan has everything I don't." Come on. The truth is that Dan is going blind. He has a genetic disorder that is getting worse as the years pass. He has to contend with depression and fear every day. Dan is so f'n brave but sometimes he can't handle his reality. And his parents continue to keep a close watch on him because they're terrified he'll kill himself, so he lives at home.

I was cherry-picking the good stuff I thought he had. I'm an asshole. I admit it. I'm humble enough to admit that I had a part to play in the most devastating breakup of my life. But, you know, I'm thankful for the experience. You're getting this book out of it.

If you get nothing else from this step, let it be this: change is possible. Be patient. The process of breaking up is embarrassing, frustrating, disorienting, and even debilitating at times. Be humble enough to ask for help. Be gracious enough to give it. Have gratitude for all that you have and all that you're supplied for.

You're doing it. You're doing a good job. Keep practicing. You're growing. And I'm proud of you. We're in this together.

Claim the grace that's here for you now by soaking in these words:

I will not hide behind my pride. I will let my barriers down. I will choose who I let in for all who come into my kingdom (or queendom) will be met with the grace that forgives all transgressions. I am no saint. That is not my aim. I am here to experience all that life has to offer me. I will not run away in fear of the things I refuse to face. I will ask with a wild spirit to be met by those who are strong enough to temper my fury with knowledge. This is not the knowledge that leads to judgments but to greater possibility. I am strong. I am a safe space. I am alchemy. I am sovereign. I am peaceful. But make no mistake, I will fight for what I love. I will not back down. I will not let darkness overcome my light. I set my sights on higher ground. I do not have to know everything — just the next thing. The rest of my life remains the rest of my life. And in this moment, I give up holding on to the memories of us as if they were a raft in frozen waters. I will die a thousand times to be reborn. And in this moment, I am on my path to freedom. I am freedom!

And so it is. Take this moment to rest in the sweet arms of Breakup Rehab.

Overcome Pride
and Grow Forward

*"The greatest thing in this world is not so much
where we stand as in what direction we are moving."*

JOHANN WOLFGANG VON GOETHE

Step 8 of Breakup Rehab is about overcoming pride and growing forward. Without forward motion we just get stuck. It's risky to love and risky to grow. I've witnessed my clients' relationships break apart because one partner will look at the other and say, "Do your work." Pride keeps us from seeing that it's "our" work. Now the real work is to use self-awareness about how pride contributed to your breakup so that you can grow forward.

This is a crucial step. Overcoming pride is the difference between repeating old patterns and creating a new life. If we keep an eye on the past it will replicate in our future. Remember, our reality is a collaborative effort between mind and matter.

IT'S NOT A RACE

Who are you really competing against when you make breaking up a race to win? Or were you racing to get your way? Either way, we tend to compete with each other only to lose sight of the real prize — creating the love we want with someone who wants it too.

Western culture prides itself on individualism, which leads to competition over collaboration. Both growth and creation are collaborative processes. If your relationship was a competition for who got their needs met most — the power struggle — then chances are that caused the breakup. We do the best we know how at the time. Some attempts are better than others. It's true, your ex may really suck at life. You may suck just a little too. You have a choice to be prideful and competitive about it or seek to work in collaboration with cooperative components — people, places, and things that contribute to your well-being.

Let me talk to your heart for a minute. *Hey, I know you feel broken right now. I know that the mind is barking orders at you. It's okay. You know what to do. That's right. Find your rhythm. You feel a little off right now. A little confused. But you know where true north is for you. Just give yourself a little time to stabilize. You've been running a hard race after all.*

I assure you, we're all unstable after a breakup. Our pride is often a major contributor to the fallout. Adam Shannon, the author of the website DeadlySins.com, defines pride as "excessive belief in one's own abilities, that interferes with the individual's recognition of the grace of God. It has been called the sin from which all others arise. Pride is also known as Vanity." I believe that vanity is the denial of impermanence in that all things will return to dust and ash in this physical world. We cling tightly to dysfunctional beliefs because of pride and vanity.

When I'm working with clients to help them through their breakups I often ask, "What caused the breakup?" Of course, there are a variety of answers, including finances, kids, cheating, lies, falling out of love, a bad sex life, residual pain from trauma, and more. Of those issues, the underlying force seems to be someone who is too prideful to let their walls down, to admit they feel shame, and to ask for help.

Pride, like judgment, blocks our growth. We get stuck and can't make the transition into healing and moving forward. I like to flip the script and bring up that a lot of people feel pride in "being unencumbered." If you date, it sounds like, "Let's just keep it casual." Well, you know, I think fear of commitment is fear to grow. What do you think?

Where do commitment issues come from?

Pride.

"But, Rebekah, what about good pride? Can't I be proud of all the things I've collaborated on? Is collaboration good and competition bad? What's the difference?" Thank you for asking, person whose voice I pretended to be right there. You can be proud of yourself for leaving a bad relationship, which is good. But you can have pride and think you're better than anyone else because you left that relationship, which is vanity.

Growth comes not in running the race against others and winning. It comes with realizing it's not a competition. You can be proud of who you are without having pride.

BEING PROUD VERSUS PRIDE

As psychiatrist and researcher David R. Hawkins explains, "Pride may take the form of over-valuation, denial, playing the martyr, being opinionated, arrogant, boastful, inflated, one-up, haughty, holier-than-thou, vain, self-centered, complacent, aloof, smug, snobbish, prejudiced, bigoted, pious, contemptuous, selfish, unforgiving, spoiled, rigid, patronizing, judgmental, and in milder forms, pigeonholing." Even if you do your very best to let go of all your old baggage, pride has a way of hanging on. Pride stunts our growth.

Pride stops us from getting the help we need. Prideful people don't ask for help. People who are proud celebrate their achievements. Prideful people boast of their achievements. Pride excludes. Being proud is inclusive. I really hope this is helping. I'm doing my best to provide you a strong foundation you can build on. Are you allowing yourself to receive it? Or is there some resistance in the form of pride still getting in the way?

You're smart. I know it. Breakups are not a measure of your intelligence. The problem with pride is that it might have you believe otherwise. That's because pride, ultimately, is void of love. It will exclude you and everyone else who doesn't measure up. Pride will say things such as, "Thanks, I can take it from here." Can you?

Remember *Sons of Anarchy* Sam from step 3? He had too much pride. We were roommates, and the first year we lived together was fine. But by the second and final year of sharing a home he was drunk every night. I would hear all six feet four inches of him come crashing to the ground in his room some nights and shake the wall between his room and mine.

Sam felt directionless in his life as a massage therapist and was trying to pass his boards to be a certified healer. He felt like a loser for being in his late thirties struggling in his career and not married. He felt like a fool for not having enough money. And he felt out of place because all his friends lived in another state. Things got increasingly tense between us because of his disposition (and because of mine — fiery Italian). Also, I was a bad roommate who didn't do the dishes. But that's beside the point.

Sam didn't know how to ask for help. He walled off his emotions and became passive aggressive. Sometimes I'd take a moment to check in with him and ask, "Are you okay?" His eyes would well up with tears and his voice would shake, but then he'd take another drink and say, "I'm fine."

I use that as an example because pride kept Sam stuck. Some of us get taught to suck it up, figure it out, and be nice but not too friendly. We should rely on our parents but not too much. We should want the love of our life to complete us but we get told to be whole first. Come on! It's tricky standing on your own two feet and being responsible for your life.

It's not all rainbows and whiskey. But don't give up just yet. We've still got some more work to do. Back to the breathing. Deep breath. In through the nose. Out through the nose. One more.

Take a snack break — no sugar. Maybe get some tea and a piece of fruit. Speaking of fruit, how amazing is it to watch a flower turn into a fruit? It starts as one thing and then becomes this luscious other thing. You're like that. Maybe you just got plucked before you were ripe. So seed in some good soil, wait for winter to pass, and grow forward.

GROW FORWARD

It's almost redundant to alter the phrase "go forward" to "grow forward." But going somewhere is not the same as growth in an intentional direction. I can go to the gym but if I don't work out when I'm there I'm not going to grow. I can go to the library, but if I don't read the books I'm not going to learn. I can go to church, but if I don't surrender all then I'm going to carry my own burden alone.

You have this one shot, right now, to turn things around. I'm asking you to trust the bigger picture. Trust in the guiding force that is destiny. There is more for you to do. More to see. More to experience. If destiny is the reflection of our decisions, and our decisions reflect our destiny, then wouldn't it make sense to decide to overcome pride so that you can grow forward?

Are you too prideful to admit that you have a strong belief hidden inside of you that you don't deserve good things in your life? What beliefs do you have that construct the foundation of your reality? Wayne W. Dyer said it best, "No one knows enough to be a pessimist." Another way to express this same sentiment is, "What are you betting on?" Do you believe that you're totally supplied for or are you focused on simply surviving? I wonder what it will take for you to grow forward?

When our relationship comes to an end our foundation gets rocked. Rather, the attachments we had to our world-view get reorganized. Life certainly changes when you go through a breakup. You can't share your day with your ex. You have to pretend they're a stranger. Some of us have to move out and find new homes. Some of us have to go back to work. The severity of the pain we feel once the shock of breaking up subsides is proportional to how attached we were to the life we had.

The gap between where we are and where we're going is where we grow. A life-coach friend of mine calls this "your growth edge." Let's say you were really comfortable in your relationship and the breakup came as a shock. Your edge is to learn how to manage being extremely uncomfortable and employ the life skills needed to weather the transition from coupled up to single again.

Some of these life skills include managing finances, cooking for yourself, using technology, socializing, net-working, and learning to navigate life on your own. Growth is about all the moments that bridge the gap between what you already know and what you need to learn.

As the saying goes, "Grow or die."

MASCULINE AND FEMININE FORWARD MOTION

We also need to grow forward through the gap between male and female. Our genders and the polarity between them affect how we go about the business of growing for-ward. I think it's safe to assume we all want to express who we really are and have someone else be really into it. We want to play king and queen of the castle. We want to be kissed and caressed and ravished. We want to be saints and sinners and have both be okay. The real trick is to want what we need. According to self-help expert Tony Robbins, men and women share six basic needs:

1. **Certainty:** assurance you can avoid pain and gain pleasure
2. **Uncertainty/Variety:** the need for the unknown, change, new stimuli

3. **Significance:** feeling unique, important, special or
    needed
4. **Connection/Love:** a strong feeling of closeness or
    union with someone or something
5. **Growth:** an expansion of capacity, capability or un-
    derstanding
6. **Contribution:** a sense of service and focus on help-
    ing, giving to and supporting others

After a breakup, I often hear women say, "Men are so…
stupid." And I hear men say, "I just didn't understand what
she wanted." Well, we both want to have our needs met.
Robbins's list of needs illustrates our commonality. Yet men
are different than women. We're wired differently. In addition, both men and women have different degrees of masculine and feminine energy within their being and body.
So while we share these basic needs the real growth comes
in the process of bridging the gap between yin and yang
energies.

The gap between the masculine and feminine can stay a
divide or it can be bridged by overcoming pride and growing forward. But, honey child, men break up differently
than women, don't they? Hold on to your genitals, there are
some stereotypes ahead.

Men choose their mates by what they see. They pick their
mates like a prize that will elevate their status. Guys fear gold
diggers because they instinctually know, deep down, that
written in the code of masculinity is the impulse to provide.
But men want to be loved for more than that. They want to
be made to feel like heroes.

When a man breaks up, when he feels he failed, when a
man gets hurt, he has a few culturally acceptable options on

how to express it — anger or sexual domination. Good job, us, for leaving those as the options. Awesome job, society. Way to go. The pain from breakup has to go somewhere, so if it can't be processed through talking, expect anger. Masculine energy is catalytic. Act first and circumvent the conversation later. Simply, men act out their emotions.

Sports provide an acceptable space for men to process emotions. When they talk about stats, they may be subtly expressing their desire to be validated. Sports conversations are code for "Do you have that insane pressure to perform inside of you too?" which sounds like "Man, look at the stats on that guy." Of course not all men do this. Of course there are men who are great communicators and leaders. There are emotionally intelligent men. But then there aren't too.

Am I getting this right, guys? I can't tell you how annoyed I get when I see women leading workshops on teaching men how to be men. It's one thing when women counselors and coaches try to help facilitate emotional connectedness and another when they attempt to teach men how to be masculine. In reference to the latter I often think, "This is like teaching a penguin to fly." Because, you know, they don't fly — so futility.

So, masculine person reading this, if there is something I'm missing about how you operate, please write me and tell me. I'm going off the data I've collected over the years.

Women, how lucky are we that we get to process our feelings by talking about them? *So much talking.* How many people have you told about your breakup? Did you post about it? Did you hire a counselor? Do all your BFFs know? I send out an f'n APB when I break up.

We talk so much. And we overthink everything.

We write lists about our ideal mate. Gag. I know that the self-helpers are telling you to do this. "Just write your list of all the characteristics you want." What actually ends up on the list are the qualities of our girlfriends. "You're talking about a man, right?" This masculine-feminine stuff is complicated. It's hard to bridge the gap without at least a few breakdowns.

In order to grow forward we must spend time getting acquainted with our masculine, get-it-done side and our feminine, nurture-and-be-nurtured side. The gap between the two can be bridged inside ourselves. We're both yin and yang energy. The right side of our body represents the masculine and the left the feminine. Focus on the integration of the two in your body and you'll start to see the growth that comes with doing that in your life.

GENERATIONAL GROWTH

What is this bringing up for you? What role are you playing in our generational growth? I hope it's making you wonder about the state of relationship. Every generation is like, "Kids these days are so stupid and disconnected. They're immoral little shits." That's not what I mean when I say consider the state of relationships. I mean, do you think there is something we could return to that would help us feel more connected? Why do we need each other anyway? A lot of people blame technology for the lack of connection. Is that it or something else? Have we lost our teachers? We tend to ignore old people, so the youth seem to be making it up as they google along.

Young adults don't know what to want. Currently they are stuck between the old paradigm of the nuclear family and fast-speed internet relationships. How do you think we're creating our lives within the current environment?

I think we're all relying on instinct. Pride is instinctual. So we're all relying on pride. This is what makes self-help so insidious. A lot of the time, it's a map back to pride. Sure, self-help talks about love — I'm ranting; there is a point — but does it get us there? Maybe, if it returns us to wisdom. But wisdom has been replaced with knowledge. Knowledge has been replaced with information. Information has been replaced with…we don't know yet. Self-help?

Were you taught how to love or is this something you knew? Was it a part of you when you came to earth? I believe love is in our DNA, encoded within us. Being human means being subject to experience. Our bodies are time-sensitive instruments. A part of us is infinite — our soul. And a part of us will die — our body. Love is infinite so it's always with us. But the part of us that will die responds to life instinctually. This split between infinite and finite, love and instinct, also contributes to our crisis of connection.

I could host a seminar on the reconciliation of body and spirit. Suffice to say, nature brings us back to love. Of all the teachers of love, I believe nature to be the best. It's always giving, providing, sheltering, supporting, challenging, and correcting. Nature is forever renewing itself. It grows and grows and grows unendingly.

What if you approach your relationships like nature? Would you be so prideful? Humans are interesting creatures. We've been given all this power that we bottle up and tuck away inside of our rational minds. We stifle it with pride. We cut ourselves off from ourselves. We stop growing forward.

So I ask you to lean in and listen to the rhythm of your heart. *It's okay to hurt. It's okay to not hurt. It's okay to be afraid. It's okay to not be afraid. It's okay to know what you know. It's okay to not know.* Listen to the rhythm. Lean in. Listen to the rhythm. Lean in. There is a pulse to your destiny and a strength in your vulnerability.

Surrender your pride. Proclaim with me now:

I am not perfect, but I will not be measured by my flaws. I will be measured by my ability to correct them. That does not mean I am right. I am not here to prove my worth. I am here to claim it. I was once lost but now I am found. I was once blind but now I see. I see that my actions had consequences. The things I did were not fair, just, or kind. I have had my fair share of abuse from others but mostly from myself for not standing up and letting the world know how to treat me. I am a child of Spirit. I am humbled by my power. I will not fear my success or make excuses for my failures. I am able to respond to the challenges that life presents to me. I will not shrink. I will not hide. I will not stop seeking the depth of my character. I will walk hand in hand with the destiny that continues to call me forward. My time has come. This is my day. I am forgiven. I forgive. I am taking action to right my wrongs and restore justice where there was injury. I surrender my pride. I am returned to love — to my original nature. All is well with my soul.

It has been said that an empty cup can't fill another. So get right with yourself. Be honest. Grow forward with Breakup Rehab.

STEP 9

Recognize the Strength in Your Vulnerability

"Being deeply loved by someone gives you strength, while loving someone deeply gives you courage."

— LAO TZU

Step 9 in Breakup Rehab is all about recognizing the strength in your vulnerability. A lot of us don't like to feel that weird drop in our stomachs that signals — dun, dun, dun — vulnerability. This could be that stage in your breakup where you've talked your friends' ears off about your ex. Or no one will go to the bar with you anymore because when "the song" comes on you turn into a pile of mush, after which your friends then proceed to make fun of you. Or if you have great friends who are totally supportive, they're still tired of your story. So you may consider hiring a counselor (ahem). In any case, I'm going to show you just how strong you really are if you're willing to step into *your* vulnerability.

I feel you. Being called strong can suck when that's not

what you want to hear. It would be nicer to hear, "This is really hard, isn't it? It's okay to fall apart. I've got you." How many of us get that response?

I hate it when people tell me, "You're so strong." To which I respond, "Is there another choice?" Actually, there are several, which land people in totally different kinds of rehab. So the fact that you're here is pretty major. It means that, at the very least, you're letting go of the idea that there is an answer to life. There isn't. We're all just figuring it out together; some more honestly than others.

Wait! Don't put the book down. Did you want an answer? All right. Wait for it…wait for it…wait for it. The things that you seek to find are unlocked through vulnerability.

We've talked a lot about being hurt by your breakup and the judgments and pride that cut you off from trusting others and yourself. So let me put in really clear terms what cutting yourself off from awareness does: it's crippling in the long run.

There are people in life who are surface dwellers. They can't dive deep into emotions and can't stand pain. It's not that they don't feel pain or feel the hurt from a breakup; they can't deal with it. In order to manage their feelings, they eat, they numb out on TV, they spend one day on a "new routine," they favor comfort over challenge. They're fat, lazy, complacent, entitled, and whatever else goes along with being a surface dweller.

To each their own. But these surface dwellers who look good on paper and in social media aren't happy. Okay, so here is the cool part of this conversation. So what if they aren't happy? Why are you paying attention to that? You're not happy, so have some compassion because surface dwell-ers don't face their fears. They run from them. Don't focus on them. If you want to be happy, if you want to feel con-nected, if you want to be a champion, then you have to be strong enough to be vulnerable.

WE'RE AS SICK AS OUR SECRETS

One of the phrases that comes out of AA that is so powerful is "we're as sick as our secrets." The more secrets we have, the more of a mask we live in. We hide, emotionally contort, people-please, manipulate, and bully. Why do we do this?

It's time for another psych lesson, this time on the in-ternal family systems theory. The crux of this theory, devel-oped by marriage and family therapist Richard C. Schwartz, is that we have three sections of our psyche: the manager, the firefighters, and the exiles. The manager is the part of us that helps us run our lives. We all have a window of tolerance. Emotions that peek outside of that window cause anxiety, and emotions that dip below that window cause de-pression. It looks like an EKG pulse mark. If our heart beats within a certain window, we're fine. It would sound like, "Ahhhh! I'm good, I'm good, Boo." The manager operates within the window of tolerance.

But let's say life gets out of control because of a cer-tain overwhelming event — a breakup. Then the firefighters come rushing in with coping mechanisms to put out the fire and get you back to baseline.

When we're in overwhelm it's often because the exiles are stirring. These are the parts of our psyche where we hid past hurts and where we keep our secrets. Some of our secrets are so hidden that we don't even know about them.

A breakup can catalyze the exiles and therefore expose our secrets. Things we haven't dealt with can bubble to the surface. The work then is to not suppress those realizations and feelings but to release the exiles through compassionate examination. This is a very vulnerable process.

Events such as rape, molestation, abandonment, neglect, abuse, and anything that threatens our body's well-being can turn into exiles. The healing comes when we integrate those experiences into our lives without fear or judgment for having had those experiences. It's hard work.

Looking at things we don't want to look at makes us feel vulnerable. It takes courage and having an open heart to heal. We humans are going to feel. Sensations keep our body alive. Hunger — feed me. Thirst — water me. Desire — explore pain. Pain — time to grow. Love — I am. Fear — figure this out. Weakness — only in my mind.

How was that lesson? Good? Did you get all that? We don't deal with emotions because, for whatever reason, sometimes we don't have the resources to process them fully and so they get buried. That is why it takes strength to be vulnerable. You must unearth the thing you thought was going to kill you.

Exiles become weaknesses when they remain secrets. It's through feeling the pain of their release that we become strong.

PAIN IS WEAKNESS LEAVING THE BODY

During my graduate school internship, I had the honor of working with veterans who served in Iraq and Afghanistan.

Those veterans taught me the phrase, "Pain is weakness leaving the body." I love it because it helps reframe pain. Rather than have it be something we defend against, it can be a signal that we're getting stronger. We're only as fragile as we believe we are.

Think about a weak person. What defines them? What are they like? I don't think of myself as a weak person, but living in Southern California makes you a little soft. You can have whatever type of food you want. You can hire someone to do just about anything for you — and I mean anything. But somehow it's never easy enough. We Botox our faces rather than drink enough water. We suck the fat out of our asses rather than do some f'n squats. And "duck lips" are everywhere. Hair plugs, fast cars, more things, status — all of this is surface bullshit because we try to correct on the outside what we aren't willing to face on the inside.

Your breakup is your rite of passage from the outside bullshit to your inner strength. Red pill. Blue pill. You can either be weak or strong. Will you set your exiles free? This is the moment you find out how dedicated you are to your path. How bad do you want it? I sound like a drill instructor. "How bad do you want it?"

Be still and listen.

Pain is a message to listen to what your body's sensations are trying to reveal about your psyche. Weakness is all the ways we resist receiving the message. When we acknowledge pain, we learn from it and free our exiles — weakness leaves the body.

Pain. What have you learned about your pain? Have you gotten close to it? Are you still avoiding it? Pain signals the places that we need to gather our strength so that we can create more of what we actually want. If you stop judging it, you can learn from pain.

Pain will touch every part of your life, especially after a breakup, if you let it. It's everywhere. "Oh, good morning, pain." "Good afternoon, pain." "Are you coming to dinner too? Okay, see you there." Everywhere with the pain! It just keeps coming around in the next relationship, and the next, and the next, until we're like, "What is it!" Then pain is like, "Are you finally ready to listen? You've been ignoring me with all those distractions for years."

Once you agree to listen to pain it will start in, "You know, you have some weaknesses in your body."

"I don't want to hear that, pain." I know, none of us want to hear that.

Pain continues, "I tried to let you know that loneliness was going to tell you to go ahead and hook up with that asshole. And do you remember when I was like, 'Don't max out your credit card trying to impress her'? Or how about the time you dated that person who I told you was all wrong for you."

In this narrative, pain sounds like an Italian mother. "But you wouldn't listen. You had to just do it your own way. And are you eating okay? You don't look good." I could go on. Are you catching my drift?

Pain sends signals through the body. The way that we respond to them makes the difference between weakness leaving the body or compounding pain in our psyche. If we listen to what pain is asking for and respond accordingly, it leaves. If not, it doesn't.

Rejection is painful. It leaves us feeling exposed. It tries to convince us, "You never had the capacity to love or be loved." We take it personally. We kick and scream. We barely pause long enough to see that we're dragging the past into the future. Everything feels laced with anxiety and filled with the abyss that is depression.

Why does it have to be so hard? Honestly, can't we all just get on a list for arranged marriages that has nothing to do with sorting through dating profiles? Again, there isn't a quick answer to fixing pain. But in being vulnerable there is an opening.

People who are successful in love understand and operate from the truth that the journey never ends. There will always be something else to train for, some challenge to conquer, and something worth fighting for. They're not special or different or have some secret formula. If there was a secret formula it would be this: listen to what your pain is trying to tell you.

One of the best ways to slow down and listen to pain is to go into nature.

ROOT TO RISE

I had the most amazing yoga teacher at Vital Yoga in Denver. Desi Springer teaches a whole new system of yoga called the Bowspring. The premise of the Bowspring is to root your toes so the rest of your body can rise from the ground up. *Root down. Rise up.* Or *root to rise.* She would say those phrases as mantras. We can be vulnerable when we're rooted, and when we do this it helps us rise out of the darkness.

In this moment, as I remind you to go into nature, you can do it right where you are. Press your toes into the ground. Feel the activation of your muscles. Engage your core abdomen muscles. Lift your chest and roll your shoulder blades down your back until your chest is slightly lifted. Do this and it will posture your body in a way that connects heaven to earth.

No matter how advanced we become as a society, there will always be a part of us that needs to return to Mother Earth. The quickness with which we have sex with another person, the pressure to "get a relationship," and the loneliness we all carry are just markers of the denial of our collective vulnerability.

As you take time to mend, go into nature. Again, get off your phone, get off social media, and go let the sun hit your face. Of all the relationships we can have, the one with nature is, in my humble opinion, the one that is best at renewing our inner strength.

INNER STRENGTH

Remember the fearless child you once were? Not in the sense that you were never scared but rather curious, inquisitive, and prime for discovery. The unknown wasn't yet something to barricade yourself against — it was exciting and full of possibility.

The comfort we get from the dream that one day we'll find the soul mate who makes us feel complete is convincing. After all, a dream is a wish our heart makes. A dream is just that. It's a wish. It's not a guarantee that when we find the right person, we'll be certain about forever. It's not a promise that we won't ever be alone or that everything will be better. Dang it!

I know I sound like an old person when I say this, but

there is only one thing of which we can be certain: everything changes. No duh. We need to be reminded of this because when going through a breakup we don't want things to change. We want to go back to how things were. It's like when you eat a burrito. You want to go back to how it tasted and not have to deal with the three-pound food baby in your stomach. Okay, I went off the rails with that metaphor.

Back on track.

It's only when we allow ourselves to be vulnerable that we get to experience our inner strength. All the steps have been leading up to this. Letting go makes us vulnerable. Trusting ourselves makes us vulnerable. Making decisions makes us vulnerable. Embracing love makes us vulnerable. So does living with purpose, being compassionate, practicing humility, and giving thanks. And it all involves change. It takes strength to bring down the barriers between you and you, to face the demons inside that say:

> *I'm not enough.*
> *There isn't enough love to go around.*
> *I'm bad.*
> *I'm failing at life.*

Raise your hand if you've felt or feel this way. Me too sometimes.

Our infinite souls want for nothing. But here we are in these bodies that are wired to survive. We pluck, bang, strum, and play each other like instruments. We step into a relationship like it was a concert hall and then fill it up with sound. Our body collaborates with another body that resonates, and two hearts beat as one orchestra. But then the music of two stops, and there is only a dull and worn-out refrain — a gasp — *love me.*

How vulnerable is it to sing your own song? To dance to the rhythm in your heart? To make up new steps as you go? That song inside of you isn't gone because your lover left. So without embarrassment, be strong, brave, and vulnerable, and let people hear you. Hear me now, sing your song.

Turn your hymnals to "Amazing Grace." The sermon is about to begin.

It's okay to fall apart until things fall back together. Vulnerability doesn't focus on what is lost; it focuses on what is possible. This means you don't have to have a plan. I really encourage you to not rush into firefighter mode. Relax. Breakups are really complicated.

One of the big wins of being vulnerable is you don't waste time employing elaborate defenses. You just begin to tell it like it is in the moment. This kind of honesty may sting but in the long run it's a kindness. Vulnerability helps you see yourself and your ex differently.

You see the world through a lens of compassion. You acknowledge that we've all been there. Since there is nothing new under the sun, we'll all get the chance to experience our own brand of love, hate, fear, and every other whimsical and terrifying emotion.

Every time we love is a reinvention. We're called back to the drawing board to etch out a new map using the instruments of our thoughts and feelings.

Vulnerability is an admission: *I feel*. That's all you need to engage life courageously and without shame. Vulnerability will guide you through the pain you feel right now. It will speak easy, feel fully, and be with you always.

In fact, pain is vulnerability's ally. Remember that it speaks to us through sensations in our body. It's sending alarm bells that hunger is about to be unleashed. Vulnerability turns toward pain with compassion and says, "I'm here. What do you have to teach me?"

FINDING YOUR STRENGTH

I really want to hear your story. I don't want to hear the details. I don't want to hear the complaints. I want to lean in and listen for the pulse that keeps you alive. I want to feel confident that you're uncovering the treasure chests of truth inside your heart. I want to experience relief as your voice begins to share these truths. I want to stand next to you, this evolving creature, and learn from your brilliance. I want to feel awestruck by the awareness that you express. I want to know I could be protected by you. I want to witness that coy smile slide across your face when I ask, "How'd you do it?"

I want to hear you say to me, "I found my strength in my ability to be vulnerable. I learned how to ask for help. I learned to be compassionate in a way that opened me up to receiving love and to giving it. I forgave my ex. I let go of judgments. I'm more focused on discovering new experiences than I'm fixated on finding answers."

I want to look back at you with wonder. There will be a softness in my face, a juxtaposition in my smile, and tears welling up in my eyes. I'll take a deep breath. You'll take a deep breath. And we'll be right here, surrendered to all of it.

SURRENDERING TO VULNERABILITY

Did you feel the intimacy in reading that? I've been in a relationship with you since you picked up this book. I told you that I would walk with you and here we are going through the steps together. I've been asking if you would be willing to surrender, to stop making excuses for your breakup, for your ex, or for yourself. I've been holding your hand and yelling at you from the sidelines.

I can't see what is in store for you. I just want you to be safe. But more than this, I want you to trust your strong heart. It knows how to tell someone, "I have to let you go. My well-being is more important to me than being with you."

Oprah says it best:

> God can dream a bigger dream for me, for you, than you could ever dream for yourself. When you've worked as hard and done as much and strived and tried and given and pled and bargained and hoped …surrender. When you have done all that you can do, and there's nothing left for you to do, give it up. Give it up to that thing that is greater than yourself, and let it then become a part of the flow.

Surrender isn't a sign of weakness. It's simply another way of saying "I know my limits." It's being real with yourself and your ego. Once you embrace the fact that you did the very best you could, there is nothing else to be done.

If you're sad because you simply can't believe that he chose something other than "us," or that she just up and left you, and if you're wishing that you could have done something else, please understand that you don't have to fight anymore. It's time to nurture your hunger with truth. Acknowledge your pain and learn from it in order to be released from it. Receive the message of strength that your destiny has ordained just for you. Ask for what you need.

When you ask for what you need, you're being vulnerable enough to reveal yourself. This builds strength because you're opening yourself up. You're setting your exiles free.

Stand in your strength by saying these words and claiming them as your own:

I am strong. I am strong. I am strong.

I continue to come to the understanding of the fullness of love. I have reconciled my past by letting it go through the active practice of surrender. My days and my nights are filled with declarations of peace, joy, prosperity, and faith. I will not let outside opinions steer my internal compass. For I am a lighthouse, a beacon, and though the waters are choppy I will weather the storm. I ask for what I need. I ask to experience more than I have ever imagined possible. My love will catalyze more loving in the world. I know that my life has meaning. I set my gaze upon a new day. I welcome pain as a messenger. I have the endurance to carry on. I will have new adventures. I will never stop learning. I will open my heart. I surrender all. I am strong.

What can be more vulnerable than being alive? Breakup Rehab.

STEP 10

Maintain Your Integrity

*"Integrity is telling myself the truth.
And honesty is telling the truth to other people."*

— SPENCER JOHNSON

Step 10 of Breakup Rehab asks you to begin to integrate what you've learned by maintaining your integrity. This is done by being true to you. But what is this "you"? Who is that? Who was that? Who are you now? An impermanent body? A permanent soul? What is going on? Okay, I get it, this is heavy stuff and you just want to feel better. Standing in integrity will help you do that.

IN THE BEGINNING WAS THE WORD

Alrighty, time for a lesson in etymology, the study of the origin of words and the way in which their meanings have changed throughout history. I'm going to add in some irrational magical theories too, because words are magical tools.

In her book *Your Word Is Your Wand*, Florence Scovel Shinn references biblical text that reminds us that death and life are in the power of the spoken word. Words have power, a magical quality. When weaved together they color our lives like paint on canvas. Words convey feelings. They're generational, and they're building blocks of our reality.

Words carry weight. They have an impact. They can completely convey the essence of who we are or they can be used to create a mask. The words we say to others are potent. The words we say to ourselves are salient. Maintaining our integrity means being mindful about how we wield our words. Be circumspect about your communication moving forward and give yourself a pat on the back for completing this short lesson. Now for more stories and such.

I had a friend who went through a horrible breakup after dating and living with her boyfriend for four years. She described him as selfish because he didn't want to get married. But she compromised what she really wanted so she could maintain the relationship — early on in the relationship he told her he wasn't interested in marriage and yet she persisted. I'm not telling you this to make her or him sound bad. We all do this when we date; we compromise so that we can make room for the other person. The issue is that we give up our integrity by lying about what we actually want and what feels true in our souls. "I want to get married" doesn't pair well with "I just want to keep it chill."

As a reaction to her breakup she started to date and have sex with all these guys who were treating her just as her ex had. Her ex cheated on her, left her with bills, and then "abandoned" her. She spent hours weeping in her room, got seriously ill, and started to run out of money. She wasn't willing to deal with her unresolved pain so it ran her life by blocking her from clearly communicating her needs. Because of this she became passive aggressive and the cycle of distressing relationships continued.

Risking your integrity for a relationship can sometimes mean risking your life. We're as sick as our secrets because the energy it takes to repress them also stops us from communicating with integrity.

This is real. Families get broken apart. Bank accounts get wiped out. Careers fall apart. People fall into addictions. Life ends when we stop being true to ourselves. I can't impress on you enough how important it is to get over your pride, practice humility, and ground yourself in your integrity.

This doesn't mean you're going to get everything right. I totally slept with my exes after our breakups. I hooked up with guys who had girlfriends only to have awkward conversations months later when they called me and were like, "Are you dating my boyfriend?" Um…no…we just hooked up. I've dated people who were like, "Yeah, I'm totally sober," only to discover after the fact they were still doing drugs. I have *so* messed up. When we don't use our words to communicate our true desires, we can really mess up our lives. We're not perfect.

INTEGRITY IS NOT A MISTAKE

Even in your brokenness you're whole. You can be a person of integrity and still mess up and break up. Integrity doesn't mean having a perfect life. Beyond clearly communicating, integrity also means being intentional and cleaning up mistakes when they happen.

Love doesn't exclude you because you mess up. It allows you to set aside your judgments. Love restores your soul and gives your body a chance to exude vitality. Your ex is not a bad person. Love is for them too. It's just as we grow forward, sometimes it's in different directions. The person that's going to be with you every step of the way is you.

We all go through cycles and rhythms. Change can bubble under the surface of our awareness for a long time. Then there is a catalyst that evokes awareness of the impending change. Our mind examines it for a while like a puzzle. It starts to form a strategy on how to bring this idea into being. Then, as if by magic, our body breaks into the exact choreography needed to manifest the plan.

Consider for a moment having to move out of your lover's home (if you lived together). That requires a plan. It requires your body to search for a new place to live, to pack, to lift, and to move there. The idea becomes words and those words manage the direction in which the body moves.

Once things are in place and a rhythm is flowing, an ease follows. It becomes second nature to maintain the new action. If amendments are needed, they don't disrupt the flow. New energy replaces old energy and nothing turns into something.

We're facilitating this flow together. By now you should have a sense that change is setting in. Even if you sat down and read this book in a day, new perspectives will be evident in the way you talk about your breakup and your life moving forward.

How to Integrate Integrity

Say what you mean and mean what you say. The bedrock of integrity is the foundation on which you need to build your life. From here on out, let's just say that, for the purpose of BRx, integrity is right speech.

Integrity, as your inner dialogue, is your internal compass. It knows how you should be treated by others and by you. It connects to the rhythms of nature. It's wise. It has an intimate connection with your destiny.

You're doing it. You're on your path. My dear, how far you've come. Every day in every way you're getting better and better. But you may also suck at some things for the rest of your life. When you drop the judgments about being better or about sucking, when you don't make them significant, you can return to the knowingness inside of you that speaks the truth. Your life then reflects you just being you.

I wonder who you are. What do you like? What turns you on and lights you up from the inside out? Why did you date your ex? What was it about them that drew you in? I'm sure I could spend hours getting to know you, but the person who needs to do that right now is you.

You can choose a few ways to do this. Take care of a pet. Be of service to a population that could use your talents. Get in a new relationship (it's an option, but you have to decide if it's a wise one). Travel. Try something new such as pottery, piano lessons, or some creative activity that is accessible. If you want to have what you've never had you must do what you've never done. Hours of motivational speeches taught me that.

Never stop learning. This doesn't mean go through life

like Animal from the Muppets — ahhhhhhhh! It means set a pace that feels good to you. Make a plan. Take action on it. Maintain it. Then add something new. Rinse and repeat. The more you do this, the more you'll get in touch with your integrity and understand how to keep it intact.

TEST OF INTEGRITY

Big life changes have a tendency to put our integrity to the test. They challenge the foundation of our beliefs and shine a light on our values. Change can push us into the abyss of endless *what ifs* and even make us take a gamble on our future.

Dating apps exist — there is no turning back. Not everyone uses them, but for those who do, integrity can feel hard to come by. After Dan, I spent some time trying to date by swiping, texting, and meeting. But after months of this, I couldn't lie to myself any longer. I didn't want to "keep it casual" with Tinder guys. I wanted more. In fact, not admitting to myself what I actually wanted was self-abuse. I had to take responsibility for my words and actions in order to stop it.

Taking responsibility for your life and owning what you create is integrity. It takes integrity to get out of abusive situations. It takes integrity to stop abandoning yourself and betraying yourself through words and deeds. Have standards and stick to them. Don't give up the goods to someone who isn't worth your time. Keep yourself in check by watching what you think and say. If you catch yourself saying, "Eh, get it while you can..." you're in trouble. I know because I've done that. It was totally beneath my integrity to have sex with men who couldn't care less about me.

Integrity keeps you on the straight and narrow path to truth and justice. Specifically, your integrity is about rising to the challenge time and time again. It doesn't mean you pass the test. Failure is a part of growth. Just be honest about it.

Integrity is about keeping your word and telling the truth. It's your intention coupled with action. Holy balls, I can't emphasize this enough. You can be the most honest person in the world but it means nothing if you don't take action on it. I don't mean act out and throw an adult tantrum, "Humph. He needs to choose me!"

Choose yourself. Kick out the crap. Know your worth and don't settle for less. Construct boundaries that work for you so that you can maintain your integrity.

One of my friends, Shine, lived this firsthand.

After Shine's divorce was finalized, she went through a dark period of drug and alcohol abuse before she finally chose to get sober. Things really started turning around when she began to date Peter, a fellow AA member.

With her new relationship Shine not only had support getting sober but she also had a partner to help support her and her daughter. Peter came from a wealthy family and worked a good job in the entertainment business. Shine once said to me, "He's into music, and that's good enough for me."

Shine and Peter were together for four years before they got married. Their relationship was full of adventure and travel — and addiction. Both of them stopped going to AA. Shine did her best to stay sober by immersing herself in spiritual teachings and seminars on flower essences, energy healing, and Reiki. As she got more adept with healing practices, Peter got deeper into partying and his old habits.

A huge component of addiction is codependency, or people-pleasing. So it wasn't surprising when Shine started drinking and partying with Peter. After each episode, she would fight to get sober again. This cycle built up resentment between them. Even worse, Shine depended on Peter for financial support. She felt trapped.

One day Shine discovered disturbing images of teenage porn on Peter's computer. When she confronted him, he brushed it off. It was then, after years of fighting, that she realized nothing was going to change. Rather than just study spiritual teachings, she began to apply them. Shine worked on trusting herself and acting from a place of integrity — and then she filed for divorce.

It's a paradox how we can watch our friends go through something like Shine did and feel righteous in our perspective but when it comes to ourselves — total blindness. You can't be clear about who you are unless you invest in self-reflection. Listen to what you say. Take stock of your reactions. Make corrections. Refine as you move forward.

INTEGRITY REQUIRES REFLECTION

Recapitulate your actions that led to the breakup. Did you make a promise to yourself that you'd never do that again, only to find yourself doing it again? What well-laid plan did you leave just lying there? Let your actions teach you something about what motivates you.

As the saying goes, "Where your attention goes, energy flows."

In other words, what's in your heart will show itself in your actions. What you talk about most and what you focus on will get most of your resources. If your actions don't deliver on the outcomes you desire, examine your thoughts.

Your actions are trying to tell you something. *Listen.*

This is the moment you reflect on the work you've done in all the steps leading up to this one. Have you been thinking to yourself, "I'm totally broken. I'll never love again!"? Or maybe you feel glad that it's over. The things you're thinking and telling yourself echo in your actions.

When you look back at your intentions, shoot for introspection and objectivity. If you want to know where you've been, look at who you are today. If you want to know where you're going, examine your thoughts. We're always evolving. Some faster than others.

If you're wondering when you'll "find love" again on your path, consider imagining who you'll be once that happens. Coax a vivid image forward in your mind. If you aren't particularly visual, write down how you'll feel in that relationship. How is who you are becoming informing who you are now?

When I was getting ready to move from Colorado to California I had this awareness: "There is a version of me out there who I've yet to meet. I'm not sure what she'll be like. I'm guessing she'll look like me, but she has some other experiences in store that I won't have if I stay in Colorado." Well, that awareness proved to be true. I moved to California, lived by the ocean, moved into one of the richest neighborhoods in the country, got a podcast producer, and scored a book deal. While all those accomplishments were wonderful, my appointment with the softer side of me was the most profound affirmation of my intuition.

MASCULINITY AND INTEGRITY

A man has a lot of responsibility to be a protector and provider. You're expected to initiate and take control. But the world is full of mixed signals. I know this because I've spent my whole adult life using masculine energy to survive. I've been told, "You intimidate men." Survival took precedent over my feminine softness.

My father, who was molested by his mother, had several affairs and dealt with his emotions by leaving home, checking into hotels, and getting drunk. He eventually died from a heart attack while having sex. This, of course, has left an indelible mark. When your father dies as mine did, you lose your compass. And when your mother dies of cancer as mine did, you lose your will to love. When you feel abandoned by life, as I have felt, you abandon yourself. All that is left is the instinct to survive.

So for years of my life the masculine side of me was charting a course of force — provide and protect. It was pushing, striving, and running. I got a lot done, but I was empty. Then, after two years in California, my feminine side began to show herself. My destiny made an appointment with the softer side of me. I answered the call to make the move. I let go, I connected with and learned to trust my authentic self, and I made a wise decision to rise up and meet with my destiny. All of this required me to be vulnerable enough to trust who I was and am becoming, to stand in my integrity.

Appointments with You

So far we have covered various ways to gain greater self-awareness so that you can live from integrity. The basics of communication that promote integrity include: use right words, manage your inner dialogue, and don't speak ill of your ex. The basics of healthy communicating after your breakup: journaling, talking to a professional, and meditating. Work in civil conversations with your ex as needed. Great. Everything is spick-and-span. Squeaky clean. But what about sex?

We still want release. We still want our nipples stimulated. We still want to feel deep penetration. We still want to feel the thrill of foreplay. We still want to indulge in the orchestra of erotic sounds. We still want to use our bodies to evoke pleasure. We still want to feel desired, attractive, and sexy. I'll be damned if your breakup is going to take that away from you. Buuuuuuttttttt, hookups are not the cure. Porn isn't going to patch you up. Web-cam girls will just take your money and leave you drunk on fantasy. Cutting yourself off from sex could have adverse effects. So what's a single person to do?

Okay, now it's time to talk about sex — with yourself. One part of your body can give pleasure to another part. How amazing is that! No shame in that. Total joy in that. Where there was a communion of two, masturbation can be a communion with you.

Masturbation is a wonderful tool for connecting with

new levels of you. I don't mean rub one out. Create a sensual setting that helps your body relax into being orgasmic. Use focused yoga-style breathing to direct the energy in your body in a way that amplifies pleasure.

Set aside time to touch, caress, stroke, and rub your body. I suggest using coconut oil as lubricant because of its many beneficial factors as well as the fact that a little goes a long way. It can be fun to use vibrators to masturbate but they also can decrease sensation over time. So it's best to stick to manual stimulation with your fingers or hand and to focus on the sensual aspects of your body, not just the stimulation of your genitals.

Doing this will help you find the rhythm of your body. Masturbation can help you quell the compulsive horniness that comes alongside your breakup, which can be a primal coping mechanism. Taking time to touch yourself will help you begin to understand how you react to your desires, how they motivate your behaviors. This connection in the moment will also make you more sensitive to when your intuition is communicating with you.

The point of masturbation as communication is not to focus on the two- to twenty-second crescendo. The release we feel when we orgasm is only a part of the whole. Integrity is about wholeness. Masturbation involves creating a setting for intimacy, touch, and exploration, and collaboration with your body. Unifying with your physical sensations can create more integrity in future communications. It doesn't have to be all about getting off. It's about building a relationship between you and your body.

If it feels good to just rub one out, do that too. But be mindful of the motivation because some people use masturbation as a distraction and not as a connection to self. The point of integrity is to be comfortable with your body so that you're not walking around in a dissociative fog. After a breakup, it can feel as if our soul leaves our body and hovers right outside of it. Touching your body is a wonderful way of coming back into the moment and learning how to ground yourself.

My podcast producer, John, always tells me, "Getting to know yourself is an inside job." Your breakup is going to bring out different sides of you. Greet them and be gentle with them. It can be embarrassing to acknowledge a part of you that you didn't realize was there. Consider each encounter as an appointment with you. It's okay. Just lean in to your wholeness, that integral part of your being. It will be your compass. It will restore your will to love. It won't abandon you. It will connect you to truth and guide you on your path.

The essence of integrity is wholeness. The actions you take from a place of integrity will echo back to you as the energies of fulfillment, grace, and pleasure.

This step is completely about maintaining what you've already put into place in the other steps so far. The foundation of creating the love you want will require integrity. To solidify this energy and all you've learned through the application of the steps, repeat this paragraph to yourself three times:

> This is my life and I will live it. If I make a mistake, I will forgive it. If I make a wrong move, I will pivot. If I stand, I will stand with integrity. I will kneel and pray. I choose me. I stand at attention at the dawn of each new day and vow not

*to take my awakening for granted. I will not slow my pursuit
of character. I will not shy away from the energy of inclusion. I
will be bold. I will be brave. I will choose to live a life where even
if the world does not know who I am, I do.*

The self-reflection that catalyzes personal development
lives in the boundaries of integrity and within the steps of
Breakup Rehab.

STEP 11

Own Your Power to Love

*"I always want to stay focused on who I am,
even as I am discovering who I am."*

— ALICIA KEYS

Step 11 of Breakup Rehab is about your power to love, so it packs a punch — equal parts sermon, dissertation, tip sheet, and tough love. Maybe you wanted to read a book that has a happy ending, where the author finds the love of her life by the end. This is not that book. That's not to say I'll be single the rest of my life. That's not to say you will be either. But right now we're going to turn the crossroads of your breakup into a bridge to your future.

The building blocks to owning your power to love are desire, dedication, discipline, devotion, decision, and don't you f'n give up! I want to be crystal clear here: I don't know if you have a shot at getting back with your ex, but if that is what you want then go after it. And let me remind you that the issues that created the breakup won't change unless you do.

So what about destiny? If you think that destiny means that your life is mapped out for you, then what are you going to do about it? Sit around like a lump on a log? Just lean back into entitlement and think that a map means you don't have to hike the trails? No. You get off your ass and you decide to do whatever it takes to be 1 percent better each day. You dedicate yourself to well-being. You devote yourself to the rituals that support your "woke" awareness. You push past the edges of your weakest self and use discipline to create a new future. Build that bridge and don't get stuck at the crossroads of despondency, disappointment, dumbfoundedness, and despair.

All that said, we don't wake up feeling powerful after our breakups. There are mornings that it's just impossible to get up. Then there are mornings where we get up and it feels impossible to find the hope that anyone will love us. Then there are mornings that are impossible to get up because we *had* someone who loved us. Then somehow, over time, we get up.

We find the motivation to go to the gym. We eat better — mostly. We start thinking about investing money instead of compulsively buying things. We do our accounting, laundry, chores, errands, and *adulting*. Laughter returns. The longing for love, well, it doesn't leave. It's my perspective that single people are the real warriors in this world. That's not to say members of a couple can't be game changers, but it's *not* the same game.

WE'RE THE WARRIORS

Being single is hard. Yes, some of it is first-world-problems hard: "Oh, poor me. I'm able to pick up and go wherever I want, whenever I want." Then there's real-world-problems hard — single parenting, paying bills, living with your parents, dealing with shitty roommates, not making enough money, coping with illness, and handling basic needs, to name a few. I've said it before and I'll say it again: "To whom much is given, much is required." Single people are 100 percent responsible for staying fit, being spiritual, being financially sound, creating pleasure, and managing life because, as you now know having been through your breakup, you don't have someone you love helping you pick up the slack. Some days it's a fight just to be a responsible single adult.

Let's really examine why it's hard to be single. First, the laws favor being in a couple. Why do you think the LGBTQ community fought so hard to be recognized as married? It's not that marriage is all that great of an institution. It's that it's one of the most recognized, validated, and supported institutions on federal and state levels. Second, it's easier raising kids with two parents and a two-partner income. It's expensive to be single. Everything costs more because you don't split it with someone. And everything costs more if you're single and have kids to feed.

Of course, several logistical factors make being single hard, but they pale in comparison to the emotional impact of being single. As journalist Rosa Silverman reported in the *Telegraph*, the nights alone, the lack of loving touch, the void in sex, the desires, the longing, and the fear of dying alone kill people sooner. Really encouraging, right?

Being isolated and single can be deadly. It's not a nice fact to deal with. So, yeah, being single is hard. But owning your power to love is how you live a longer and more fulfilling life. We all bloom at different times in life. Don't be hard on yourself for your breakup. Remember, there are worse things.

One of the tragedies in life is spending it with someone who doesn't care about you but keeps you around anyway. I've heard it said, "It's better to be single and want to be married than to be married and want to be single." When you get really desperate after years of being alone or after just breaking up, it's easy to think, "I'd rather be in a bad relationship with someone than in this crap relationship with myself by myself!" If you feel this way, please see steps 1 through 10 now. They're all meant to curb that kind of thinking because it's not true.

Your self-esteem is up to you. It feels good — necessary, at times — to be validated. But an infinite being doesn't need validation, and a part of you is infinite — your authentic self, remember? As long as you're here on earth, the work is never done. When it's done for us, when we expect love to save us, when we forget what we incarnated for, then we give up our power. Stop that. Take ownership over your life. Align with your destiny.

Even if destiny has determined "the person" for you, you still have to get there. You still have to do the work. You still have to take control over your bad thoughts and bad behaviors. Fix them. Get right with you. Apologize to those you hurt; take a cue from AA and make amends. Be grateful for what you have been given. The gut punch that is your breakup is meant to build your character. You've got the love you need to see you through. Own it!

WHAT IS OWNERSHIP?

Ownership means to have authority, dominion, sovereignty; to stand in faith, to exist in a sanctified space, to claim, to declare, to proclaim, to affirm, to be in command, to rule, to acknowledge, to admit as fact, and to possess. With these words in mind, consider then what it means to own your power to love. It's a bold act. It states that although the world is hurting, although there is pain, and although you feel all of it in your bones, you will not stop loving.

Let's do a lesson in music because musicians have created a lot of content around what love is, what it does, how it feels, and, honey child, the heartbreak associated with it. What is love when the thrill is gone? Does love lift us up where we belong or bring us a higher love? Can't we help falling in love when there ain't no mountain high enough? And what if we just have crazy love? I know you're like, "Straight up now, tell me." But I'm not going to tell you what love is because love can't be defined. Love can only be experienced. Just remember that ownership means "you've got to express yourself!"

In closing this lesson, go ahead and make your breakup playlist. You're going to survive because wild horses can't drag you away from the stairway to heaven. If love is a battlefield even when it's all we need, how do we let it be? We change the world with our own two hands. And when we get that feeling, we need to remember to ask ourselves, "Where is the love?" Rock out with your heart out.

I told you I was going to preach. I've given you a lot of different ideas to ponder. I've offered you some things you could try so that you can feel stronger. You might feel like,

"This is great and all but I still want my ex back." Or you may think, "Will any of this really help? It kind of seems as if saying this stuff about love is obvious. So how is this going to actually help me?"

I get it. I've heard a lot of bullshit in my time. Plus, I don't like being told what to do or how to think. That being said, integrating this idea — I am love therefore love can never leave me; I cannot be separated from love through pain or loss — was my resurrection. I own my power to love!

Owning your power to love is an affirmation of your life. I spoke to a woman who was in an abusive relationship at twenty and got out of it at twenty-two. She had gone to therapy with her abuser and the therapist didn't identify that she was in an abusive relationship. Instead, the therapist offered clinical solutions to a systemic problem, which was a problem.

Nonetheless, this woman was able to get out of the relationship and felt inspired to start a Facebook page addressing the issues of domestic violence. This resulted in an outpouring of people asking for help, which inspired her to start a nonprofit. She took ownership over her bad situation and through the power of self-love turned it into something that helps others do the same.

Challenges make us stronger. They can shape how we respond to life and who we become. But ownership over your life doesn't have to be only inspired by trauma. If you invest in self-development and remain curious about the meaning of your life, it's possible to fully embrace the talents you were given, express those talents fearlessly, and rise above the noise.

Owning your power to love doesn't mean tempering your voice. Rather, it means you learn the pacing and cadence at which it's best received. You learn how to command attention rather than demand it. You learn how to be magnetic rather than forceful. You understand that perfection is not the destination; the flaws and the cracks, the rivets and the holes are what make up the beautiful mosaic of your unique life.

It's all poetic. It can be tragic. And there are some logistics to work out. Up to this point I've talked about breakups but have not addressed divorce, which would be stupid to leave out of *Breakup Rehab*. So in the next sections I'm going to address what owning the power to love looks like when going through a legal breakup. I'll also go over how to have a healthy relationship. In this way, you can have a clear picture of what your life is like and what it can be like if you work with the steps to create the love you want.

PICK IT, PLANT IT

Here is one of my favorite sayings: *If you like something, you pick it. If you love something, you plant it.* Well, breakups have a way of ripping up lives from the roots. This is especially true of divorce. I was a part of a divorce collective, which is a group of professionals including family lawyers, judges, social workers, and therapists who get together for lunches and talk about helping clients create parenting plans, divide assets through arbitration or mediation, and prepare for custody agreements. It was all very complex and somewhat heartless. I asked one of the lawyers if they provide emotional support to their clients who fall apart in their office.

He simply replied, "No, I just try to get information to build a winning case."

Divorce is a legal breakup. Taking the official position to get married means you'll likely have to assume a contentious stance to end the relationship. This is especially challenging when there are kids involved. The power to love seems to turn into the will to win. It's human nature. Divorce has a way of helping us get acquainted with our dark sides — some more evil than others.

Again, as the lawyer I talked to alluded to, divorce is a cut-and-dry process from a legal standpoint. It's just a matter of negotiating terms, settlements, and conditions. However, we all know that vowing forever and then being part of the 50 percent who weren't able to make that happen wreaks havoc on our psyche, health, and bank account.

So how do you survive a legal breakup? Again, take ownership over your life — handle it.

I've been down a few dark alleys, so to speak, and I know what it takes to bounce back. First, you have to admit your shortcomings. Second, get clear that there is a part of you that is unshakable. Third, take good care of your body — it's just trying to survive. Fourth, connect to a social network that will support you with unconditional love (BRx support groups can be started anywhere — maybe you start one). Fifth, get your spiritual practice on point. Sixth, work the steps. Lastly, give it time. Of all the things you'll go through in life, time will be the cure-all — time brings and time takes away (Job 1:21, BRx adaptation).

It may take your whole life to accomplish creating the love you want. I can't think of a more worthy venture. So give yourself all the space and time you need to heal. Then, one day, you will love again.

HEALTHY LOVE

It might be too soon to date. In fact, that is exactly what I watch people reach for after a breakup — the next person. So when we talk about "loving again" I'm not suggesting you date or have sex anytime soon. That being said, if destiny has someone in store for you, who am I to tell you what to do? *Carpe* that fucking *diem*.

Lean in, honey, I'm about to get really real with you and tell you a story that demonstrates "owning it." I went to Naropa University for graduate school and Beth was in my program. We became besties. Well, my bestie and I had one thing in common — dating losers.

Because we were both genius enough to work out our daddy issues through dating, we were a bit reckless. She got pregnant. I got herpes. Goddamn it! Let me tell you, we both have learned the hard way about who the good men aren't.

So Beth, my friend, hooked up with this guy. She thought he was "sooo different." Then she calls me, "Rebekah, I'm pregnant and" — let's call him *dickwad* — "dickwad wants nothing to do with it. He even wrote me a letter telling me to abort the kid. My career is ruined. I'll be fat and ugly for life…" It *was* ugly.

Well, Beth endured the pregnancy alone. She had her healthy baby and spent the next year in court fighting for child support, doing paternity tests, and arguing for her child's rights. In the meantime, she was trying to get her therapy practice up and running.

Let this be proof that the old idea that you have to be perfect to help someone out, to have it all figured out, is the dumbest idea on the planet. I think the best counselors are the ones who live this shit. And Beth and I have lived it!

A year of fighting went by. She finally won all her court battles. The next day she got on Match.com. Within three dates she met "her person." They have been together for two years now. It's not a happy ending. They have a lot of life to negotiate in their relationship. And they're making it work. But Beth was brave enough to own her power, fight her battles, and love again.

When it comes to loving again and being with a new person, STIs (sexually transmitted infections) can be a real sore subject. As far as herpes goes, one out of four people have it in one form or another. Some below the belt and some above it. It's the source of many comedic jokes. Just know if you're having sex, condoms can only protect you from so much. Herpes is a skin-to-skin communicable virus. I think the worst part of the virus is the stigma that goes with it. People with cold sores don't fear that the other person won't have a relationship with them because of the virus. But if I have it on my bits, well, damn me to hell. It's ridiculous.

I also know I risk being single longer because I shared this. But you know what? Fuck it! The truth will set you free. Honestly, herpes is a rash that can be managed by doing what you should do anyway — eat healthy, avoid drugs (coffee being one of them), and exercise. It's not an abusive *dickwad* of a man who tells you to abort your baby. There's a difference!

When it comes to partnership, I've found that people

who want to get to know me for me are willing to learn about how to be sexually safe with me, both emotionally and physically. That is what you want. You want someone who will care for you. When loving again, be honest about your health when it feels healthy to do so. And for a good time, own your power to love.

HEALTHY RELATIONSHIP

As much as I've been like, "Uck with the online dating, that shit is terrible," it works. People meet people that 50 percent stay married to. I'm not saying *not* to try it. Destiny isn't really picky about how it gets what it needs to be delivered to you. The trick is learning to listen to what your gut and your heart are telling you. "Hey, you up there! Head! We have some things to tell you. Ugh. It's not listening. Well, let it make the choices. We'll just use pain to get its attention after this whole thing goes up in flames."

Our internal communication is like this, I imagine. The head makes all the choices (the little one, too) and the heart and gut clean it up by making wise decisions. The minute we tune in, like, really listen to our heart and gut, our intuition immediately strengthens. We're more adept at connection and connecting to our unique destiny.

Your health matters. Invest in it. Start and continue to work out, eat right, drink enough water, get enough sleep, avoid drugs, go on vacation, go into nature, and do those things that light you up from the inside out. In addition, you're going to need to learn how to have a healthy relationship.

Have I not taught you how to do that yet? Okay, here is the tips list on how to do that:

1. **Learn to communicate your feelings.** You have to be vulnerable in order to do that, which includes feeling your feelings. Cliché, I know, but true nonetheless.

2. **Make wise decisions by setting firm boundaries** with how people are to treat your body, heart, and mind. Be discerning about the situations that you get yourself into.

3. **Teach people how to treat you.** If you're an asshole to yourself, *stop it!* Would you treat a kid the way you treat you? "Hey kid, you're stupid and fat and no one will love you ever again." If you said yes to that, you're a bully. Catch my drift? Be nice to yourself.

4. **Don't date losers. Risk rejection.** Ask people right away what their values are. If they don't know what values are — run. Run away and never look back.

5. **Use sex for connection instead of instant gratification.** Sex isn't a dirty thing (and STIs don't make you a bad person). It's something our bodies do. In the right context it connects us to our authentic self. Only a slut could tell you that and know what she's talking about. So, you know, maybe listen to this one especially. Save yourself for the person who loves you back.

6. **Get to know yourself.** Access you through spiritual practices that work with you.

These are the six basics of creating and maintaining a healthy relationship. There might be some things I didn't include that you and your authentic self can figure out. In any case, I hope I haven't confused you by saying, "There is no answer. It's not all up to you. This thing called destiny has your life written out for you. But you have to take ownership."

It makes sense if you trust this one thing: there is a force greater than you guiding your life. It lives in you and moves through you. Remember, destiny has dominion over your direction. You have dominion over your body. Knowing this helps you own your superpowers.

Own Your Superpowers

We all have superpowers. Some of us know what they are. Others don't or they don't believe in "those things." In order to tap into your superpowers, I invite you, in this moment, to widen your perspective. Step back from the troubles, anxieties, and issues in your life. Now take a deep breath. Keep widening the space between you and things that bother you by breathing deeply and slowly. Creating this spaciousness is the requisite for claiming your superpowers.

The next step is to become a witness to your life and the events as they unfolded, and to take an inventory of how you show up in your life. One of my superpowers is being mom-like. I didn't realize this until I had an event that made it impossible to miss. I joked before about dating losers. I've also been told, "You can't save people." Yet somehow these sad and broken men (echoes of my father) kept coming into my life.

For a while, I beat myself up with the questions, "What am I doing to attract these guys? What's wrong with me?"

Then it clicked. When men are awful to me, I get nicer. When they're sad, I want to cook them a meal. When they really disrespect me, I wonder how they're hurting. I began to review how I showed up over and over again in each relationship. And I began to recognize the person I was showing up as was an Italian mother. She loves with her whole heart, cooks nutritious meals, provides shelter, and doesn't run away if you disrespect her. My actual Italian mother would also lose her shit, which I've also done.

In any case, one of my superpowers is to love like a mom. Who do moms tend to care for? Kids. Of course, we want a partner who is nurturing. We often pick people who emulate our parents. But when it comes to my choices, I now know that I don't have to choose losers to rescue. By *losers* I mean the people who represent my disowned parts that I'm not willing to look at. Love is a mirror and self-reflection is a potent superpower — I said reflection, not obsession.

Again, I invite you to review who you were in your past relationship. Were you the damsel in distress, the hero, the loving mother, the provocateur, the loving father, the protector, the provider, or something else totally unique to you? We all carry traditions in our DNA that result in repeating family patterns. It's when we examine those patterns and make a decision on how to take ownership of them that we can change them.

Mastery over your life is a superpower. To live your one unique life. To forgive. To walk your path with purpose. And to claim your power to love.

When you do these things the ache from loss transforms into an ache to give. It's not that you don't have what you want. It's that you have so much, you're so full, and you're so grateful that you feel compelled to share it with the world and to grow it inside the boundaries of a loving relationship. Answering your unique call to service is one of your greatest superpowers.

Service Is Power

What does it mean to be of service? I'll tell you what it doesn't mean — being a martyr. Being of service isn't the same as self-righteously giving of yourself to your own detriment. Being of service is fully expressing your unique gifts and giving of them for the joy of doing so. In this way, you're a living blessing, as you're blessed.

The more you listen to your heart, the more aligned you are with your calling and the more joy you bring to your life. Being part of a couple is dynamic if both parties seek to be of service to the other. But most of the time we start to think, "What can you do for me?" This is why taking time to know what lights you up from the inside out is an important step to feeling and being powerful. When you know what you have, you can be clear how you can give to another.

Explore your gifts. Do you cultivate them or do you ignore them? What crashes down like a wave on your imagination and sweeps you out to sea? Now is your chance to fall in love with *you*. Why not see just how far your bliss will take you?

Owning your power to love is a form of mastery. It takes experience and perseverance to become a master in love and relationship. I've reminded myself that a flat stomach, a million dollars, and a true companion all take time, and it's the kind of slow work where the results show up in one big burst. Every little decision over time accumulates to create what can seem like overnight success. You're on your path. You're doing it! You can't know what you didn't know until you know that you didn't know it. So be easy on yourself but don't be lax. You've got important things to do and more to learn. Keep growing forward.

I understand that the road ahead is long. For every ending that feels like a death in your life, there will be a rebirth. Nature shows us that for every winter there is a spring — cue The Byrds' "Turn! Turn! Turn!"

Everything you're building toward will be delivered to you at just the right moment. I know from experience how hard it is to believe in a tomorrow that hasn't arrived yet. I also know that everything we want or need will arrive if we ask for it.

Connect with your power to love now and declare these words:

> I have the courage to live the life I was destined to live. I have come to do and be more than to follow along and follow "the rules." I do not have to keep doing what I have been doing. I can and will choose again. I can change one degree at a time or revolutionize my whole life and start in a brand-new direction. I have a life and love that most people cannot begin to imagine. I will find a way or I will make a way. I will rise up. I will raise my standards. I will inspire those who come into contact with my heart and soul. I will grasp opportunity and persist day after day. I have the grace to conquer my doubt,

fear, and ignorance. I am the hero of my story. I am the victor. I choose love and loving from a place of possibility. My life is not an accident. I am strong and willing to embrace all that I am and all that I will be. I will. I am. I can. I have power within me!

Love on with Breakup Rehab.

STEP 12

Create the Love You Want

*"We must be willing to get rid of the life we've planned,
so as to have the life that is waiting for us.
The old skin has to be shed before the new one can come."*

— JOSEPH CAMPBELL

Step 12 of Breakup Rehab is about creating sacred space, honoring your journey through the steps, acknowledging how brave you've been, and focusing on applying the skills you've learned to create the love you want. In this step we set you up for success in love and in life. We review where you've been, encouraging self-reflection as a habit. We look at where you are, taking inventory of the moment. And we anchor you in your unique path.

Recovery takes time. It's hard to slow down enough to listen to the still, small whisper inside that calls you to something greater than yourself. But now is the time to use the BRx steps to claim your role as a powerful creator and ride a wave of victory. Now is the time to drop your judgments. Now is the time to accept what *was* and to be with what *is*. Now is the time to awaken to a world where you know how to create the love you want.

CALL LOVE IN

Look at your life now. It's a product of your thoughts and reactions to those thoughts. For instance, one of my pet peeves is when I text someone, especially a love interest, and they don't text back. I'm like, "You have to be kidding me! It takes, like, no seconds to reply." Plus, thanks to the book *He's Just Not That Into You*, if a guy is like, "I'm busy," then I think he doesn't like me, I'm a loser, I need to fix myself — shaaaaaaame. I have that thing where if I shame me first then maybe it won't hurt as bad when the guy I like bails. It's like, "You can't reject me; I rejected me first!" It's so stupid. I know my inner critics — my firefighters — are just trying to protect me.

But what we resist persists. If I focus on not being rejected, I get more rejection. That doesn't mean people don't love me. It means I've created a habit of rejecting myself that creates the feeling of being abandoned that then loops into a self-fulfilling prophecy because I react by being needy, controlling, and clingy. "I want a needy, controlling, and clingy partner," said no person ever.

If destiny was a character, it would observe this behavior and be like, "Dude, she's doing it again. I designed challenge into her path so she would grow but, daaaaamn, she's going dark with it. Whatever. I guess I'll just hold off the good stuff until she snaps out of survival mode and remembers she chose this life, until she remembers that she's a powerful creator."

One of my mentors is Esther Hicks. She channels the spirit of Abraham. She, like many of the thought leaders I listen to, is on YouTube. A primary tenet of her message is that 90 percent of what is going on is in vibrational reality; it has not yet been translated into physical reality. Our thoughts and points of view are part of vibrational reality. People often ask Esther how to manifest more money, more love, and a better life. She delivers the same message, "You can't get there from where you're focusing." In other words, we tend to focus on our physical reality as if it was an oath or vow for what will continue into our future. "Well, I always seem to attract the same type of person, so I guess I'm doomed." "Well, that's how I was raised, so I don't know any different." "Well, I just broke up with the love of my life, so I guess I won't ever get what I want."

First, love doesn't have a timeline. Our culture does. We think that twenty-six is the age to get married; have a career by twenty-eight; have babies by age twenty-nine; change careers by thirty then again at thirty-five. These are arbitrary numbers. If you look back in history people got married at age sixteen. The point is, we focus on how "it should look." Then we start to feel bad about our life when it "isn't going according to plan." Screw that!

Second, like attracts like, meaning negative points of view generate negative outcomes — if nothing more than for our bodies. Hellooo…every stress study ever done says stress has a negative impact on the body. Breakups are stressful. They send our bodies into survival mode — fight, flight, freeze, fuck, or faint. But you — the you who observes you — can control your responses to stress through biofeedback, guided visualization, and focused breathing, and by being humble enough to learn from your mistakes.

Third, your breakup doesn't define you, Boo. Do you know how many breakups I've been through? Breakup might start defining my public persona, especially since I wrote, like, the best book ever on the subject. But this book, my life's work, and the men I date or the one I marry don't define me. I'm a force of nature and so are you. You have seasons, you'll shift and change, and you're not your experiences. *You're the channel for energy to come into being.* You take a formless thought and turn it into reality. Too woo-woo?

Okay, think of making a peanut butter sandwich with honey and bananas coupled with a cold glass of raw milk — *mmm*. I know some of you may be allergic to, like, all of those ingredients, so substitute accordingly. Now go make the sandwich. Did you have to bake the bread? Did you have to harvest the peanuts and smash them into a delicious spread? Did you transport the bananas from a farm to your home? Did you raise the bees to make the honey? Now think of all the cooperative components that support you turning a thought into reality.

I wonder what energies, people, and cooperative components want to support your healing and moving forward immediately. I wonder what else is possible.

INVENTORY THE MOMENT

Holy crap, you're magical. Get that through your head. Your soul wanted something more than to be in your relationship. If you initiated the breakup you may be like, "I didn't want to hurt my partner but they were just never going to change — or whatever." If you got dumped it may feel like, "Uh, no, I wanted to be in it but my ex wanted out and there is nothing I can do about it." Really? Nothing? I'll tell you what you can do: inventory this moment.

I love that Tony Robbins says, "Life can change in a moment." All the great thought leaders and influencers have a phoenix story, where they rose from the ashes. Wayne Dyer, neglected orphan. Oprah Winfrey, poor girl in Mississippi. Tony Robbins, abused by his mother. Eckhart Tolle, homeless. Les Brown, lived in his office building. Elizabeth Gilbert, divorced. Any celebrity ever experienced a breakup. And I love the saying, "Your setback is the platform for your comeback," which has been credited to Steve Maraboli.

You know what they all have in common? It took one decision, one moment, to change their lives. Tony Robbins has shared that overcoming the fear of scarcity with fierce faith was his moment. Wayne Dyer was guided to write *Your Erroneous Zones*, a book that stayed on the *New York Times* bestseller list for sixty-four weeks. No one who dares to be victorious avoids the struggle.

You can either focus on the struggle or you can focus on what you're going to do about it. Come fully into this moment. You still have breath in your lungs — and OMG, if you died just now this doesn't apply. Stop making your pain significant. "Oh, he did this and it hurt me so bad…" "She was just a selfish bitch…" "I chose him because I wanted to please my parents…" or whatever is looping through your mind about how much of a victim you are because of the breakup. Even if you were abused, you may have not chosen to be victimized but it's your choice to stay a victim. Stop it.

In fact, a classic cognitive-behavioral pattern interrupt is to put a rubber band on your wrist and snap it when you catch yourself thinking negative thoughts. Choose differently, and the only place you can do that is in the moment. Right fucking now. Swearing is also a pattern interrupt, by the way. So, goddamn it, stop fucking around lamenting the past, dig deep inside yourself, call your shadows into the light, invest in self-development, exercise and eat right, and stop wasting your time with someone who doesn't want you anymore or who was never going to fit the path you're on! It's go time!

ANCHOR LOVE

I totally just yelled at you. That is what a good friend does in order to snap you out of the haze that goes along with a breakup. Dating someone else right away isn't going to help if you haven't done the work — and continue doing the work — to walk your path. Buying new clothes, injecting Botox into your face, getting fake tits, buying a faster car, maxing out your credit cards, and whatever you try to fix on the surface won't help you create true love.

As a counselor, I've worked with strippers and escorts (sex workers are often the gatekeepers between shadow and light). These individuals have unique insight into human behavior. They see under the surface. I've heard it said that "the more money a person has, the more lies they have as well." Now, this isn't true of everyone. But coming from people who work in the underground world of sex work and who hear confessions on a daily basis, who hear every kind of fantasy, has made me believe that many of us hide from the truth.

Self-help author Debbie Ford has said, "What you can't be with won't let you be." What do you do to release what is lurking in your shadows? Follow this formula that I call "Tools for Creating":

Visualization: The process of organizing your imagination into expectation, which turns into an invitation for thought to transform into reality.

Journaling: "I once was afraid of _____. But now I give thanks for _____." Fill in the blanks and write as if they're fact.

Meditation: Be with your breath. Quiet your mind. Connect with your body.

Prayer: Come humbly before Source Energy and ask for help.

Burning Letters: Write everything down that is holding you back or keeps you stuck. Then in a safe place, burn the letters and say out loud three times, "I am released from the pain of my past! I am free!"

Get a Guide: "When the student is ready, the teacher will appear" (Lao Tzu).

You can return to "Tools for Creating" over and over again. Make them habit. Build rituals around them.

Another important journey to healing after your breakup is telling your story.

TELL YOUR STORY

Mexico honors the departed in a beautiful tradition known as Dia de los Muertos, or Day of the Dead. According to Mexican belief, a person can experience three types of death. The first is the death of the body. The second is when the physical shell is returned to the earth. The third is the ultimate death, when the departed is forgotten. Dia de los Muertos celebrates the dead so they will not be forgotten.

In a similar way, it's important to tell the story of your past relationship. After a breakup, we feel an overwhelming sense of loss — not just the loss of the relationship but also the feeling that we had no impact at all, that we've been forgotten. Remembering and giving voice to what happened is an important part of recovery.

Telling your story will connect you with your emotions as well as your truth. So tell it. Speak of how you met and fell in love, of your struggle and doubt. If it happened, tell of your abuse or neglect, of the fear-driven decisions you made. Revere whatever difficult lessons and hard-fought battles you've endured.

Memories of your breakup may feel like shrapnel in your soul. Like a soldier, honor those hard-earned wounds. Let them be a private source of strength while you recover. When memories of your ex creep into your mind, don't push them away or mistake them for a sign that you're stuck or failing. Know that fond memories are reminders that you're a loving person. If someone dies who once loved you, it's not wrong to imagine they're still proud of you. In the same way, rather than focus on the absence and void created by no longer doing this or that with your ex, embrace your fond memories as reminders of your ability to have fun and be loving. Highlight your ability to love — to give and to receive it.

It's important to know how to tell your story, and who to tell it to. Times of transition can put all types of relationships to the test. Know who your friends are. They'll care for you while you recover. They'll listen to your story without caring if you cry. They'll tell you when to take a shower because you're starting to stink. Seek the comfort of friends, but don't rely on them for answers. Only you know, deep down, what is true for you. Take sound advice but don't take it personally.

Of course, you're sensitive enough to know that everyone has their own life to manage. You're mindful of people's time. If there is no one to listen, journal. Write about your breakup — in essence, tell your story to yourself. Why? Because the most important part of telling your story is to tell it so many times that the emotional charge fades. Eventually it just becomes a string of facts.

Talking with a counselor is also an option for telling your story. A counselor can be a priceless tool in your breakup recovery. They can be fully accessible to you in ways that your friends rarely can. I've hired many different counselors over time to help me through the course of several life transitions, including breakups. As a counselor myself, I knew how much it could help me. And because I'm a live human being, it did.

If therapy is out of reach, then reach instead for a simple guide to meditation. Meditation can help you learn how to be with yourself, an important component in the breakup recovery process. But don't misconstrue meditation for relaxation. Stuff is going to come out of "storage." Many people are unaware that meditation can sometimes cause great discomfort. But this too can be woven into your tale.

This is the moment when you reestablish a bond with your heart. Nurture this connection by telling your story. In doing so you let go of what was, embrace what is, and allow for what will be.

Good job! Gold stars and blue ribbons for you!

You're worthy of love. You matter beyond your actions. Your existence has already changed the world. Take what you've learned and give it as a gift to those who long for true companionship. Shine your light on the world. Love has been with you always, and it always will be.

TIME IS ON YOUR SIDE

The next and most profound relationship you can experience after a breakup is the relationship between you and time. There is no substitute for time. It's a force unto itself. Recovery takes time. Let me say that again. Recovery takes time. It also takes practice to understand the twelve steps in BRx. It takes time to put the steps into action.

There is no way to expedite your recovery. It will be what it is and it will take all the time it needs. A new relationship won't thwart old patterns, so don't bother trying to skip steps in recovery. Don't allow distraction to be your medicine because it won't trick time. If you deny your feelings in the moment, they'll just reemerge at a later date and take the time due to them. When you find yourself trying to make things other than they are, you're hampering your own healing process. You can't skip steps.

Take a moment to recall how many times you've requested more time or less time for whatever reason. How many things have you wanted to speed up or slow down or simply stop? What was it all about? When it concerns a breakup, it's about love's course of healing and its relationship to time.

After all my breakups, I wished that things would speed up. I wanted to feel better so I could meet Mr. Right. He didn't show up. Instead, I got Mr. Right *Now*. There was always plenty of him to go around, and not one of them became my husband. This need for speed was just a mental construct I built around the idea that my heart didn't have the capacity to break. I didn't have time to fall apart.

Except that everyone falls apart — whether it's a little or a lot — after a breakup. The thing about time is that if you fall apart long enough, things will eventually fall back together. In recovery, it's imperative that you allow healing to take its course.

MILES LEFT TO GO: DOUBT, URGENCY, AND FEAR

Every day that goes by after your breakup is full of possibility. As you fall apart, you'll notice all the areas of potential you've left unattended in your life. Maybe you've been meaning to paint, write a book, start a business, take a trip, or let that one person know how you really feel. Look beneath the surface of your breakup. Look deeper still. Now is your chance to strip off those layers of uncertainty.

In doing so, be warned: your recovery will be challenged by doubt, urgency, and fear. These are the land mines that can blow up your fresh starts. They will make you feel as if a fresh start is out of reach. But it's not if you remember that "the only way out is through." Again, you've got the love you need to see you through. Don't doubt that.

Using Doubt

Think of the time the seventeenth-century philosopher Descartes pondered his own existence. As the story goes, he noticed a stick jutting out of a stream. It appeared bent, but when he pulled it out of the water it was perfectly straight. This led Descartes to question his perceptions, and it helped him arrive at his most famous quote: "I think, therefore I am."

When we doubt ourselves, we think, "I doubt, so I don't know." Do you talk to your ex again or do you just cut them off? Do you date or do you wait? Do you join a commune now or later? There are so many things to sort through after a breakup. Of those things, feeling solid in your ability to link up your heart and head is one — like, the major one.

This Morse-code type of communication happens when you're getting to know yourself after a breakup. It's made up of dots and dashes of what being responsible looks like while simultaneously feeling crazy. In this way it feels like "I am what I think" more than "I think, therefore I am." Simply, our minds are filled with doubts.

Doubt has the ability to manipulate your perception. In the context of your breakup, doubt will whisper in your ear, *maybe.*

Maybe he'll come back.

Maybe the breakup was a mistake.

Maybe I should call.

And then…

No more *and then*!

It seems impossible to move forward with grace and ease when doubt presses in on you. Peace is hard to come by when doubt overwhelms your sense of assurance. Doubting yourself is a horrible feeling. It can burrow at the very root of your existence even as it undermines your ability to be persistent.

Doubt creates a terrible, wounding war between heart and mind. *If I can't get what I want, what's the meaning of life?* Your mind is logical. In the face of opposition or confusion, it will compute and spit out viable answers. Your heart writes the code. And doubt? It's the virus. When troubleshooting a challenge, doubt will overheat your system, forcing an immediate shutdown. (Shout-out to the geeks, nerds, and dweebs!) This can make you panic, and once that feeling sets in you start treating everything as if it's urgent.

Urgency: Give It to Me Now!

If someone is rapidly losing blood due to a traumatic injury, that is urgent. When they gave us my mother's hospital bill totaling $1.6 million and we didn't know how much longer she had to live, getting her to sign the bankruptcy papers was urgent. Going to sleep and waking up to your house having been bombed as you scream and search for your family that is buried under the rubble is urgent. Having your sister die in your truck as you're driving her home from the hospital only to revive her enough for intensive care to keep her alive one more day is urgent (which is the tragedy that brought Dan and me together briefly). I offer these examples to help you put your pain in perspective. Your life isn't over because of your breakup.

I've given you a little tough love right now. Believe me, I know how much breaking up sucks. It's even worse if you get cheated on. If you're in an abusive relationship, leaving it is urgent. But short of it causing a total body shutdown, your breakup isn't urgent. So I encourage you to return to using the tool of focused breathing to bring you back into this moment.

Push your toes into the ground. Look left and right. Are you safe? Are you supplied for? Is your body under attack? Reorient your consciousness. Remember that although destiny has dominion over your direction, you have dominion over your thoughts, feelings, and behaviors. If your body was a boat, your mind is the captain and your emotions the sails (or motor — whatever). Just calm down. Root to rise.

I think the burden of relationship is knowing how to intelligently respond. One person sends bits of data: "You're hot. Let's hook up." The other person is like, "Ha-ha. No." This is all happening over texting, by the way. Then there is some back-and-forth. This can lead to a little hanging out. The hanging out can lead to dating. Some "meeting of the other significant people" rituals. Then your bodies hang out for a long time in this thing called a relationship, and they get used to each other; comfortable. *Oh, and then it happens.* We get that feeling, "I'm getting annoyed by the things that used to turn me on." Then someone in the relationship starts to think of the future, a life with "those" behaviors. Then we use sex to "make it better." But "it's not changing." So we break up. *Poof!* Just like that — splitsville.

Do you know what happens when we take something

away that our body has become accustom to? We freak out. Again, everything feels urgent. Now stop for a minute and consider the pressure we put on ourselves to find "the right fit" after breaking up.

"Oh, gurl, there is someone out there for you. You just have to be patient." "Don't worry, bro, you'll find the right girl." "It's okay, honey, you'll find the one for you." But, we're like, "I want it right f'n now." Sigh.

I'm particularly amused by people who think they're clever enough to "be over it," like, three days after the breakup. "No, I'm good with it." Of course, a part of us can be, but our body has to go through an adjustment period. And no one knows adjustment periods better than old veterans.

I hang out in bars with old guys sometimes — love those ol' 'Nam vets! — and they start talk'n about love. They tell their stories of good women who kept them on track. But the ones who are too prideful to admit that breaking up hurts often say, "The best way to get over someone is to get under someone else, as soon as you can." It works, some of the time. But when you have sex with someone as revenge or as a cure for your broken heart, you're not really being kind to the person you're having sex with.

There is a saying in counseling, "Victims are violent." The pain inflicted on the victim gets passed down to the next lowest person on the totem pole. In the context of breaking up, I think we pass down the pain to the next person we have sex with. And urgency cuts us off from communicating clearly. We may say, "Let's keep it casual." But we're not saying, "I feel really hurt and let down by love. I didn't get my needs met. I'm still learning how. So could we just take this slow and be friends first?"

If you're doing that — hey, man, great job! But chances are there are still some major fears invading your psyche in shifts. So don't let urgency be a stumbling block where you react from fear. Chill. Take a knee. Breathe.

The Fear That You Don't Matter

Is there anything more crippling than feeling irrelevant, useless, and cheap? A breakup can make us feel all of that and more. It can collude with doubt and urgency to make us believe that we simply don't matter anymore.

We choose people out of the fear that we'll be an outcast if we don't have a partner, that we'll die alone, that we won't be able to have kids, that we had a kid and now have to be a single parent, and for a lot of other well-intended reasons that have unintended consequences.

When you apply the BRx steps you can transform all adversaries — even doubt, even urgency, even fear — into allies. We have fears because our bodies are wired to survive. To get past this, we must use the life hack of mindfulness. It helps us face our fears and learn from them. We can use fear as a tool of refinement. We fear the unknown, so do the work to figure out what you don't know. It just takes time, practice, and a continued application of awareness.

RELATIONSHIP REHABILITATION

Breaking up is a recovery process in that it's not just the breakup that needs rehab. It's the whole way we do relationships in our modern age. We still seek to be saved by our partners. But there is no great escape. This life is a journey. We learn as we go.

As you move forward, know that you aren't wrong for your breakup. You just make choices and then more choices. Be brave and try again. There are good things ahead.

Sharing a life with someone is awesome. Morning sex has to be one of the best experiences ever. Starting a family is miraculous. Dreaming big dreams and traveling the world together are fantastic. Having "your person" in your corner creates more ease. Touch. Sex. Companionship. A confidant. An adventure buddy. The other half to your whole. Giving and receiving love in a healthy committed relationship. Yes. Yes. Yes. I'll have that. These are reasons to go through BRx, so that you can have that too.

I'm so proud of you for taking this journey with me. I can't thank you enough for your work in the world. I can't wait to hear your story and how BRx played a role in your recovery. You're beautiful. You're wise. You're so very loved.

In honoring the original twelve steps that inspired BRx, I'd like to close the steps with the Serenity Prayer:

God grant me the serenity
to accept the things I cannot change;
courage to change the things I can;
and wisdom to know the difference.

Thank you for being a part of Breakup Rehab.

Life Beyond Breakup

Okay, before you read this, cue up Frank Sinatra's "My Way." Press play. You know, my first car was a remodeled 1955 Chevy Bel Air. It was my introduction to the classics. Given my roots, I can't help but want to close with a classic song. It's time, baby. We're facing the final curtain on this journey through Breakup Rehab together. I want to tell you, there is life beyond your breakup.

I'd also like you to cue up a song from Disney's *Aladdin*, "A Whole New World." Trust me, you're headed in a whole new direction. To assure you of this, I'm going to make sure to fill your tool belt with tips and tricks. Breakups impact several areas of our lives including finances, careers, where we live, self-esteem, friendships, social media accounts, sexuality, and identity, to name a few. So before this book gets thrown onto the self-help stack, before you put it on the shelf, and before you go have sex with someone, let's run through some lists, advice, and other stuff that will help you move forward.

WELL-BEING

When you run in hippie-dippie, heart-centered, creative circles as I do, one tends to pick up a few tools to help get the mind right. I encourage you to use these tools for well-being as they apply to you.

Let's get your mind, body, communication, sexuality, and all the other good stuff in life firing on all cylinders. Go time!

Burn Baby Burn

First, you need to flush out the nonsense that is clogging your mind and blocking your heart from receiving. In order to do this, set a timer for ten minutes and write down in a letter all your negative beliefs. Don't worry about taking up the whole ten minutes. You can write one word and then reflect on it for ten minutes if you like. I did this exercise and it made me realize how pissed off I was that my sexuality had been so demeaned over the years. My pussy is magical and I was allowing people to treat it like garbage. And that meant I carried around a lot of anger about being a sexual object. It was a revelation for me and I invite you to do this as well. Who knows what you will discover.

When the ten minutes are up, burn the letter. Of course, you can do this alone, but I recommend gathering at least one other person to join you in this process. Now, I understand this may not feel like a very masculine thing to do. You may resist writing your negative thoughts down. I don't give a damn about your resistance and neither should you. Seriously, what is the big deal? Just set the timer and do this (ASAP)!

After you're finished burning the letter, take a few breaths. Root to rise. Press your toes into the ground, soften your knees, roll your shoulders down your back, lift your chest, lift your chin, and inhale. Hold. Exhale. Now place your hand on your heart. When energy is cleared away it creates a vacuum, so it's important to fill that space with positive affirmations.

With your hand on your heart say aloud, "I am powerful." Then follow up with a few rounds of "I am _____" and speak of yourself in the affirmative. After you feel complete in your affirmations, simply close with a prayer. Bow your head and say, "May I be free from suffering. May all beings be free from suffering. And so it is."

Another good exercise is to film yourself saying, "If you really knew me you would know..." and share what comes up for you. I've found that this exercise helps me get to the root of my blocks and blind spots. You can also complete these sentence stems:

"If I had no money and no needs I would be..."
"What my body requires is..."
"If I never met my ex I would be..."
"My soul's desire is to..."

If you can find a partner to help you facilitate this process, that is even better. If you can't, I encourage you to film yourself completing these statements. Pick one as the prompt and fill it in over and over until you feel a lightness wash over you.

For example, "If you really knew me you would know I feel like I can't be who I want to be so I make up roles to play so that I fit in." We often operate from conclusions. The notions that we're ugly, unlovable, and outcast can distort our connection with truth. Flush out your negative thoughts by putting them in a letter and burning it. Follow up with positive affirmations about who you actually are. Overcome resistance. Don't make it significant. Process your pain by using sentence stems to release it.

If you find these exercises extraordinarily difficult to do, get professional help. I'm so glad you took the time to read *Breakup Rehab*; individualized care may truly be your next step. Let's go through the checklist of how to choose the right healing guide for you.

Getting a Guide

I want to honor going through a breakup when you're broke. I know the internet can be a relatively free resource to help guide you through the pain. Maybe that's how you found *Breakup Rehab*. All that surfing takes time, which will most likely result in only partial answers and subpar solutions. Social media likes and comments don't have the same impact as consulting with a mental health professional. I know the argument: "That's so expensive." But if you're making $30,000 or less a year, there are clinics that provide support and practitioners who take insurance. I like to use PsychologyToday.com's directory to find a therapist who may seem like a good fit. Some therapists offer free consultations — at least I do. If you're making more than $50,000 a year you can afford therapy. Budget it in.

Here are five things that are crucial to know when getting professional help:

1. Make sure you can invest at least three months to a year working with the same mental health professional, spiritual advisor, or relationship strategist.

2. Investigate the results the counselor has when working with your specific issues. You can even ask them, "What outcomes have you seen?" Keep in mind that they can guide you but you have to put in the real effort to create your ideal outcome.

3. You can't predict the process of therapy. It's going to look different than you expect.

4. Confidentiality extends to everything you share unless you're homicidal or suicidal or if you report elder or child abuse. In such cases, confidentiality is waived.

5. A mental health professional's rate reflects their years of training, which means it's not the same as talking to your friends and family.

Alternatives to talk therapy include life coaching, massage therapy, energy healing, and, of course, exercise.

Get Your Body Right

One of the things you can do for yourself immediately after your breakup is dial in your diet and exercise routines. I know everyone jokes about eating ice cream after a breakup. I know a lot of us head for the booze to drown the pain. I know a lot of us say, "The diet starts tomorrow." But real nutrition always starts today. So give yourself a twenty-four-hour window to eat and drink what you want. Screw it; make it a party. "I've got breakup cake soaked in bourbon at my place. Come on over." But when the hangover wears off, start chugging lemon water. Down some roasted dandelion root tea to flush the liver, B vitamins to metabolize sugar, and probiotics to get your gut right.

They say that most of our health issues can be traced back to our gut. In fact, it produces more serotonin than the brain — I learned that in my graduate program. After you get your supplements dialed in, make a ten-item grocery list. You live and die by this list. Consider it your break-up-cleanse list. You don't have to stick to it forever. The only extras you buy are spices and good fats (coconut, extra-virgin olive oil, and clarified butter). An example of an excellent post-breakup ten-item list is:

1. Mushrooms (organic portobellos if you can)
2. Whole grains (brown rice, red quinoa, or farro)
3. Green veggies (kale, broccoli, bell pepper, zucchini)
4. Salsa (no sugar in it)
5. Eggs or whatever vegans eat instead of eggs
6. Chicken breast (or whatever vegetarians eat instead of chicken)
7. Fresh fruit (lemons and limes are kings)
8. Nuts
9. Raw milk
10. Organic coffee

I'm not a nutritionist so, of course, consult your health-care provider if you have health complications. But any doctor will tell you, "Make healthy life choices." Buying your own groceries and cooking for yourself are healthy life choices. I'm not here to suck the joy out of eating out. I'm a foodie, so I get it. But singles tend to treat restaurants like cafeterias. You waste money (that you could invest in a mental health pro), you eat too much sugar and salt, and your portion sizes are too large. Dial in your diet.

It's going to take some getting used to — your diet and your new life without your "person." Rather than screw around with your time and pretend to be busy with swiping, be productive by working out.

I was a personal trainer for three years, so I can speak directly to what you need to do immediately after your breakup to feel better right away — cardio and squats. I love/hate both of these. Cardio is boring as shit, and squats take every ounce of grit to get through. If you're a lazy person, this is going to be even harder. Again, I don't care about that. Do it anyway. You need to get over your mental blocks about working out. "I'm too depressed," "I'm too busy," "I don't know what to do." Just get it done.

We all know how to jog. We know what shoes to wear to jog. So jog already. Start by jogging around the block. Then improve by 1 percent each day. Run a 5K if it calls to you. Of course, if you have health complications seek advice from your healthcare professional. But if you don't, what's your excuse?

Ask for help. Personal trainers often give free intro sessions at gyms, and there are gyms that cost ten dollars per month. Also, you can do body-weight exercises such as burpees, jump-ups, jackknifes, and jumping jacks. If you don't know what those are, use YouTube to find out. Then do them and don't just waste an hour watching YouTube videos (unless they're the ones I made — ha).

As far as workouts go, I love hot yoga (once a week), dancing, lifting weights, and hiking. I also love sex as a workout. I know that you're going to miss that. So let's talk about what you can do about that.

Sex after Breakup

Sexual energy is creative life-force energy. Orgasm is when your parasympathetic and sympathetic nervous systems are activated simultaneously. We need release and excitement to feel the peak of pleasure. How do you do that if you don't have your partner to do it with?

Sex doesn't have to be all about intercourse. I know some of us opt for casual sex as a way to cope with our breakup. Some of us try to have revenge sex or just one fling (a few flings) with your ex after the breakup. That will reverse your recovery. So start to think of sex differently. What if you just allowed yourself to be turned on by the things you love?

Denver, Colorado, turns me on. I'm getting excited just thinking about the Denver Art Museum, Sassafras American Eatery (Southern cook'n), and just how beautiful parts of downtown are contrasted against the skyline of the Rocky Mountains. I loved living in Colorado. The food, the art, the people, the events, the music, and the seasons were all so sensational. But I left there because I didn't want to live in the same city as my ex, Dan.

I ended up moving somewhere even more beautiful, but it doesn't have the same feel. I share this because breakups can make us forget all the things we love. The memories we created with "our person" can cloud the joy of experiencing our favorite places without them. So when it comes to feeling that sexual energy course through your body, don't let grief steal it away by cutting you off from the things you truly enjoy.

In fact, claim them as yours.

When it comes to actual sex after your breakup, well, let's talk about that too. Casual sex is rarely casual with a stranger because of STI concerns and attachment issues. Some of us have friends with benefits to turn to. Some of us left our relationship for someone else, so there is no gap in get'n some. But if there is a gap, it can be bridged with masturbation and make-out sessions.

Before you decide to hook up, do your best to clearly communicate where you are. "Hey, I just need physical affection and for us to use protection." Sexually transmitted infections are a fact of life if you're having sex. Be responsible: get checked often, use condoms, and be real with where you are in your process of recovery.

Sex is really awesome, but it becomes less awesome if you spread it around. Again, when we overindulge in things that are meant to be sacred and special we turn the profound into the mundane. I encourage you to channel all your frustrated sexual energy into diet, exercise, creative outlets, and the spiritual practices that are right for you.

Spiritual Practice

Yoga is not just some nifty way to get a better butt. It's a devotional practice that knits mind, body, and spirit together. The simple flow of a sunrise salutation can take years to master. You must be mindful of the balance of weight on your feet when standing, the splaying of your toes, the activation of your leg muscles, the arch of your back, the rise and fall of your breath, the tightness of your jaw, and the holding of your hands in prayer position over your heart. All this goes into just standing in mountain pose.

Yoga has deep roots. Of all the spiritual practices, it's the one I recommend devoting your life to. Just learn how to do a proper sun salutation. Begin your day by facing toward the sun and flow through the movements. Of course, if you have the money and time, find two instructors you love and go to their classes. Become their devotees. Dive deep into the yogic tradition as it works best for you.

In addition to committing to a yoga practice, incorporate guided meditation into your life at least once a week. I find the best guided meditation is the kind that focuses on balancing your chakras, the energy systems in your body.

I know that yoga and chakra balancing may seem too foreign to some. So if nothing else, go to church, temple, or a house of worship and pray. I absolutely adore Catholic churches for their aesthetic. I like some of the Catholic traditions such as lighting a candle as a symbol for prayer. I often pray, "Dear Lord, please help…" If you don't know how to pray, just kneel, bow your head, and ask for the help you need. Be diligent in your prayers and, in their own way, they will be answered.

What if you're praying to get your ex back? If it doesn't happen, does that mean prayer doesn't work? No, it means that you're being brought into right relationship. It's time to remember that God is your supply.

Right Relationship

Right relationship exists when *all* parts connect us to Source Energy. What do I mean by "right relationship"? I don't mean a "perfect relationship." I'm not talking about being right or wrong. I *am* referring to a union of souls, to integrity and divinity, to being in communion with Source Energy (God as you understand him or her).

A client once asked me, "Can an unhealthy relationship become healthy?"

I replied, "It takes two factors: willingness and work."

If you stand in your power, you won't stay in an abusive relationship. If you trust yourself, you won't tolerate lying. If you want a family but your partner doesn't, you'll adjust your ideals and trajectory according to your truth.

Many relationships end because people max out their capacity to communicate. I didn't want to end things with the Dan, but I chose to end it anyway for the betterment of the whole. I couldn't figure out how to effectively communicate my caring, and he couldn't reciprocate it. Being together caused us more harm than good.

Abuse — verbal, mental, or emotional — is an absolute reason to end a relationship. Allowing yourself to remain in any relationship that makes you feel bad more often than good will keep you stuck.

Right relationship happens the moment you commit your life to your own unique spiritual journey, when you allow your destiny to summon your potential. Just like everyone else, you have a gift to give, a calling. Your relationship will be shaped by that calling.

In right relationship, you not only have the support of

your partner but also the support of the relationship itself. The relationship helps both of you become more of who you truly are.

If your bed is empty and you wish your lover was by your side, give your gift of sorrow to the world. Give what is true, alive, and vibrant inside of you. Be in right relationship with your emotions.

I'm all for doing what you have to do to pay the bills, but don't let the bills distract you. Thwart distraction by giving your gift. Get gritty and dirty with your gift. Have a relationship with it.

When you're in right relationship with God then you'll have unwavering faith that everything that comes to you will arrive exactly on time. There is life for you beyond your breakup. God is never late.

EXPERIENCE FREEDOM

When clients come to me for counseling, I often ask them, "What brought you here?" Inevitably our conversation will turn to their goals and stories about the menacing issues they face. It's good to know what led to the breakup, but that's just part of it. The next part is to ask, "What will be the sign of liberation?" How will you know when you've set yourself free?

All the steps in Breakup Rehab are designed to lead you to the answer. Breakup Rehab is an invitation to consciously engage in your recovery. It's calling you out on your calling. It's the first of a thousand steps you'll take on your unique journey. These steps also ask for circumspect acceptance of your spiritual path.

Take impeccable care of your body. It's your lifelong partner.

It's up to you to create the love you want in your life through your actions. Get clear on what you want through introspection.

Your relationship was a gift. It *is* a gift. Breaking up is just ripping the wrapping paper away so you can see what's inside.

I'm here with you. We all are.

Today is a new day, and every day after today will also be new.

Breathe in. Breathe out.

Take it one step at a time.

Notes

Introduction

Page 9, "*It is not the things we run to that restore our souls* ": Baya Voce, "The Simple Cure for Loneliness," TEDxSaltLakeCity, YouTube, October 7, 2016, https://www.youtube.com/watch?v=KSXh1Yf NyVA.

Step 1. Let Go and Forgive

Page 17, *Harville Hendrix's Imago therapy*: Harville Hendrix, *Getting the Love You Want: A Guide for Couples* (New York: Perennial Library, 1990).

Page 20, "*There are people who can walk away from you...*": T. D. Jakes, "Let Them Walk — Bishop T. D. Jakes," YouTube, June 8, 2011, https://www.youtube.com/watch?v=Pketb6gxR3w.

STEP 3. MAKE WISE DECISIONS

Page 43, *The brain has three parts*: Peter A. Levine and Ann Frederick, *Waking the Tiger: Healing Trauma* (Berkeley, CA: North Atlantic Books, 1997), 265–66.

STEP 4. FACE YOUR FEARS WITH LOVE

Page 49, *facing your fears with love*: Speaking of learning, the psychologist Erik Erikson created a stage theory for how people develop through life. In his studies he found that love is the virtue we learn between ages nineteen and forty. We have a little over two decades of our life to choose intimacy over isolation. And isn't that what fear does to us? It isolates our thoughts, feelings, and genuine self-expression. Wikipedia, "Erikson's Stages of Psychosocial Development," https://en.wikipedia.org/wikiErikson%27s_stages_of_psychosocial_development.

Page 57, *One of the great tools of our time is the five love languages*: Gary D. Chapman, *The Five Love Languages: The Secret to Love That Lasts* (Chicago: Northfield Publishing, 1995).

Page 58, *"Some people will have two or three marriages in their lives..."*: Esther Perel, "Rethinking Infidelity: A Talk for Anyone Who Has Ever Loved," TED, March 2015, https://www.ted.com/talks/esther_perel_rethinking_infidelity_a_talk_for_anyone_who_has_ever_loved.

Page 58, *Some dating sites have even built in code*: Annalee Newitz, "Almost None of the Women in the Ashley Madison Database Ever Used the Site," Gizmodo, August 26, 2015, http://gizmodo.com/almost-none-of-the-women-in-the-ashley-madison-database-1725558944.

STEP 5. LIVE YOUR PURPOSE

Page 63, *But we don't really know where thoughts come from*: Alan Watts, "Thought," YouTube, July 2, 2011, https://www.youtube.com/watch?v=by4qqGRrQ8Q.

Page 69, Emotion *comes from the Latin* emovere: *Online Etymology Dictionary*, s.v. "emotion," accessed March 26, 2017, http://www.etymonline.com/index.php?term=emotion.

Page 70, *Collins tells the story of a POW named Stockdale*: Jim Collins, *Good to Great: Why Some Companies Make the Leap...and Others Don't* (New York: Harper, 2001).

STEP 6. EXAMINE YOUR JUDGMENTS,
RESPOND WITH COMPASSION

Page 75, *Buddhists adhere to the philosophy*: Jonathan Landaw, Stephan
Bodian, and Gudrun Bühnemann, *Buddhism for Dummies* (Hobo-
ken, NJ: Wiley, 2011).

Page 76, *"Faith is belief in the right things…"*: "The Seven Virtues,"
ChangingMinds.org, accessed April 9, 2017, http://changingminds
.org/explanations/values/seven_virtues.htm.

Page 85, *He begins his show with*: "Daily Affirmation: Stuart Under-
Prepares," *Saturday Night Live*, Season 16, 1991, NBC.com,
http://www.nbc.com/saturday-night-live/video/daily-affirmations
-ii/n10026?snl=1.

STEP 7. PRACTICE HUMILITY AND GRATITUDE

Page 90, *Humility simply means you have nothing to defend*: David R.
Hawkins, *Letting Go: The Pathway of Surrender* (New York: Hay
House, 2014), 139.

Page 99, *Patterns create blueprints*: Lisa Wimberger, *New Beliefs, New
Brain: Free Yourself from Stress and Fear* (Buckinghampshire, UK:
Divine Arts, 2014), 33.

STEP 8. OVERCOME PRIDE AND GROW FORWARD

Page 104, *"excessive belief…"*: "The Sin of Pride," Seven Deadly Sins,
accessed April 9, 2017, http://www.deadlysins.com/pride/.

Page 106, *"Pride may take the form of overvaluation…"*: Hawkins, *Letting
Go*, 138.

Page 109, *men and women share six basic needs*: Tony Robbins, "Do You
Need to Feel Significant?: The Need to Feel Important and Why
It Makes You Sabotage Your Own Success," TonyRobbins.com, accessed April 9, 2017, https://www.tonyrobbins.com/mind-meaning
/do-you-need-to-feel-significant.

STEP 9. RECOGNIZE THE STRENGTH
IN YOUR VULNERABILITY

Page 117, *The crux of this theory*: Richard C. Schwartz, *Internal Family
Systems Therapy* (New York: Guilford Press, 1995).

Page 126, *"God can dream a bigger dream for me…"*: Oprah Winfrey,
"Oprah Winfrey Master Class, Surrender," https://www.youtube
.com/watch?v=rpwW42HVZws.

STEP 11. OWN YOUR POWER TO LOVE

Page 145, *the nights alone*: Rosa Silverman, "Stay Single, Die Younger, Say
    Scientists," *Telegraph*, January 12, 2013, http://www.telegraph
    .co.uk/news/health/news/9796903/Stay-single-die-younger-say
    -scientists.html.
Page 150, *BRx support groups can be started anywhere*: Find other
    people who are going through a divorce or breakup, have them
    buy the book, start a book club–style meeting, meet in person,
    potluck style, and go over the steps. Reach out to me for further
    instructions.

STEP 12. CREATE THE LOVE YOU WANT

Page 167, *Self-help author Debbie Ford has said*: Debbie Ford, *The Dark
    Side of the Light Chasers: Reclaiming Your Power, Creativity, Bril-
    liance, and Dreams* (New York: Riverhead Books, 1998), 85.
Page 173, *Having your sister die in your truck*: In memory of Jamie.

About the Author

Rebekah Freedom McClaskey can best be described as respectfully irreverent. Her life's work is to facilitate freedom. She is a relationship specialist who guides her clients to find their purpose after a breakup. Rebekah combines her psychic gifts and her clinical experience as a counselor to create true-to-life strategies that result in clients living full and satisfying lives. Her private counseling practice focuses on guiding her clients to be masters of their destiny. She lives in Rancho Santa Fe, California. Contact Rebekah via her website: RebekahFreedom.com.